Preaching In Pain...

By Evangelist Danielle Williams-McCord

Preaching In Pain

The Danielle Williams-McCord's Story Copyright © 2020 by Danielle Williams-McCord

ISBN: 9798632441964

All rights reserved. No part of this book may be reproduced or transmitted in any form or by any means, whether electronic or mechanical; which includes photocopying, recording or by any information storage and retrieval system without permission in writing from the copyright owner.

Printed in the United States of America.

Meet The Author

Evangelist Danielle Williams-McCord

Preaching In Pain

Acknowledgments

Introduction

Ch.1- Why Me?..1

Ch.2- No Support!..12

Ch.3- Church Folk..21

Ch.4- Where Is Jehovah-Jireh.................................31

Ch.5- Love/Lust/Infatuation...................................37

Ch.6- Persecution..78

Ch.7- Judas..97

Ch.8- Spiritual Monsters...137

Ch. 9- Saved & Suicidal..154

Ch.10-But God..173

Ch.11- When I Thought It Couldn't Get Any Worse...It Did..185

Letter To The Minister With A Broken Heart......203

Acknowledgments

First giving honor to God who is the love of my life. I literally wouldn't be able to breathe without him. Everyone has their own personal with relationship with God, but I happen to be a little obsessed with him. I am determined to please him by any means because I made a vow many years ago in a dark dirty basement, and I will honor that vow until the day I die. I pray my ways always please the Lord and that he is happy that he chose me.

To my loving husband Ronald McCord, who I adore. Loving me isn't always easy, not just because of my mood swings lol, but being with a woman with such a deep past and an even deeper future is not a task for the average man. You have supported me through every success and failure, every good day and bad day and I am forever indebted you. Thank you for choosing me as your good thing.

To my Bishop, my father and at times my friend Anthony Pigee Sr., I love, respect and admire you for many different reasons. Beyond being my covering, you have fathered me in the spirit as well as in the natural. You recognized my gifts and calling years ago and have made sure I walked in who God had called me to be. I publicly honor you sir.

To my real friends and family who have been with me through the storm, I say thank you, I appreciate you all. To my right hand as I call her, Melissa Horne; God knew you were exactly who I needed to help carry this vision. You are so much more than an armor bearer and an assistant, you are my God ordained sister and I thank you for all that you do for me and DWM Ministries, but what I am most grateful for is your loyalty and genuineness to serve the Kingdom.

Lastly, to every demon, devil, soothsayer, witch, warlock, psychic and psycho that tried to take me out, I thank you for your efforts. The attacks, the warfare and the hidden agendas grew me up in the spirit. It showed me how to war and defeat my opponent, which means I'm going to come for hell and everything in it every time I open my eyes!

Introduction

This book is for every Apostle, Bishop, Prophet, Evangelist, Pastor, Teacher, Armor Bearer, Praise & Worship leader or anyone serving in ministry on any level. I was led to write this book because the assignment that God has given us is undoubtedly hard and difficult at times; and it is exceedingly rare that we get to express that. In fact, we are guilty of parading around like everything is perfect as if we are unphased by the continuous attacks, when that is obviously not the case. Even as advocates for Christ, we still suffer from loneliness, depression, anxiety, betrayals, health scares, personal demons and the list goes on. When we are faced with those scenarios, it's harder for us to deal with them and we know how to mask it because we're not supposed to let people see that side of us. We are the "strong ones" if you will, so how dare we have a moment of vulnerability. We are the leaders, encouragers and motivators, God forbid the leader be broken.

I just couldn't take it anymore. I had to say something because this appointed position can be painful, and it needs to be addressed before we see more suicides amongst leaders. We are constantly pouring out to others, but who is pouring into us? For far too long, we have been running on empty. People seem to misjudge us because we have titles in front of our names, but they often forget that we are human too and I don't say that as an excuse to live in sin. We are human too, as in we cry, we hurt, we get frustrated and angry, we have feelings as well. Even Superman had to take his cape off at times.

This is my third book and all of them have been addressed to a specific group of people. **From Porn To The Pulpit** was written to give hope to the sinner. **Barren** was written to give confidence to the infertile. Now, **Preaching In Pain** is to give support to the anointed. I'm speaking to Clergy. I'm not speaking to many, but to the few who have been chosen and called inside and outside of the pulpit. My aim in writing this book is to share the truth about the agony that your "yes" may bring by telling my story, my experience and my pain. I want to let other brothers and sisters in leadership know that you are not alone. What you feel is what all of us who answer the call feel. Saying yes to God and walking in your Kingdom purpose is not a piece of cake. This is indeed a hard journey, it'll cost you somethings, it'll bring you to your knees and make you question everything, but for those of you who are ready to throw in the towel, don't!

I have quit ministry 7,891,387 times in my head, but every time I get ready to walk away God grabs me by my collar. Not to mention, I keep having Jeremiah experiences when I say I will not make mention of his name, it feels like fire shut up in my bones. Situations occur and I want to run away and rebel like a teenager, but he always does something that warms my heart again. He always reminds me of who I am and who's I am. The assignment is rough, but the Lord is gracious, loving and will push you when you feel like you don't have the strength to stand. He did it and still does it for me, so He will do it for you. Oh and just in case you were not aware, let me be the first to tell you that you can't quit even if you wanted to!

Chapter 1- Why Me?

By now, my past is no secret. The first book I wrote entitled, *From Porn To The Pulpit* goes into details about my previous life choices and experiences; which included drugs, alcohol, lesbianism, prostitution, stripping, pornography and the list goes on. So, you can imagine how I felt when I got "the call" to ministry. I thought if I was hearing anything call me, it had to be demons or the boogeyman, this couldn't be the good Lord calling an ex-pornstar to preach. My first emotion was shock. My first action was to run. My first question was, why me? For a second, I thought that I was going crazy because I kept having visions and dreams of instructions

Preaching In Pain

from the Lord. I saw myself on a platform in front of thousands of people. I kept hearing the word ministry and then these weird church people started telling me I was chosen by God to do a mighty work for the Kingdom. I thought to myself either they are on drugs or they are just as crazy as I am. It just didn't make any sense to me that this great and wonderful God would bypass all of these "good people" who haven't really lived a full life of sin or done anything horrific in their lives, (let them tell it,) just to choose a hood, emotionally damaged, stripping, sexed out, cussing, fighting, wig snatching wretch like me. At that particular time when God was on the mainline ringing my phone, I was in church heavily, but I cursed like a sailor, I had every part of my body pierced, I didn't want to be bothered, I just gotten rid of my gangbanger boyfriend and I didn't like people, so who was I going to minister to? Yet and still, I got the call.

Not only was my past not so squeaky clean, but my present situation was messed up. Even after I left the porn industry, I still had issues. I was jacked up. First of all, why would God want somebody with so much baggage? Somebody with a raggedy reputation and somebody who was ready to tear church folks up? I was emotionally unstable and not in any position to lead and yet I still got the call.

Last time I checked most Preachers have degrees; be it Associates, Bachelor's, Master's and or Doctorate, any kind of seminary training, but I didn't even grace the stage at my high school graduation because I dropped out. All of these immaculate, educated men and women of God who are available to do Kingdom work, but God chooses a high school dropout. How can I teach people when I don't even know? I had very little natural education and zero spiritual training, but I'm supposed to be a Minister of the Gospel? Not once did it ever cross my mind to go to Seminary or take any Theology classes and yet I still got the call.

I'm not saying every Minister or leader was a virgin before marriage or that they haven't had multiple sex partners because I know that is not the case, however, I put the icing on the cake! Fornicator was my middle name, and it should have been tattooed on my forehead with a big red letter "A" for adulteress and "P" for prostitute stamped on my chest. I took my hoeing nationally and internationally and although I was paid well, it left me with a bad reputation, but I still got the call. My reputation as a stripper, escort, and porn-star should have been enough for God to cast me away, but he did the exact opposite. Unlike people, instead of pushing me away, he pulled me in closer. Instead of letting me go, he held on tighter and I couldn't understand why me. He obviously saw something in me that I couldn't see in myself.

If you look at it from man's perspective, there is no way that a person, whether male or female should be able to preach the Gospel let alone lead people into a spiritual journey, clean living and holiness coming from the lifestyle I previously lived. Why? Because (from man's perspective) Minister's, Pastor's and leaders are supposed to be blameless, without sin and close to perfection; and if at one-point sin was in their lives, it couldn't be nearly as bad as mine. It's okay if he used to smoke weed and cigarettes. It's okay if she had one child out of wedlock. We can accept those small flaws, but hell will freeze over before we accept a Preacher who used to be a porn-star!

I took that into consideration, along with my obvious fears and flaws and I ran like the wind. I heard the call, but I was playing hide and seek with God hoping he wouldn't be able to find me. I convinced myself that I wasn't good enough and the Lord made a mistake when he called me. He must've dialed the wrong number. Every now and then I would view my porn movies, not for sexual gratification, but to remind myself of how undeserving I was. It would literally disgust me and make me sick to my stomach as I watched myself engage in activities that I am ashamed of; and because of my participation in the porn industry, I knew I was not fit for ministry. It didn't matter how many dreams woke me up in the middle of the night, it didn't matter how many Prophets confirmed that I was called, I refused to do what God was calling me to do, which is ultimately rebellion, however hate, judgment and unforgiveness is worse when its coming from within and nothing from the outside can compare to it. Self-hate and unforgiveness is a real thing amongst the body of Chris.t It's one thing when people dislike you and won't forgive you, but when you don't like you, that's a different kind of fight.

As a result of my "no", which was plain old disobedience to God, every door was shut in my face. My life started falling apart. I got fired from my job, my living situation became unlivable because my roommate and I suddenly didn't get along anymore. My friendships were failing. It was one thing after another, and I knew what was causing it. I felt like Jonah and I was in the belly of the fish for trying to go against the instructions of the Lord. My "no" had backfired, it was working against me and it seemed like I was on punishment.

After I came to terms with what was happening it was like the Lord gave me a reality check. He said, "After all that I've done for you, you are refusing to do what I have called you to do? You could've and should've caught diseases, been in jail and died, but I spared your life because of the plans I have for you. The enemy tried his best to devour you and I raised up a standard against him every time and now you are boldly telling me what you're not going to do. How dare you! The only reason you are still breathing is because you have a purpose to fulfill and you will do it or go back into the world and die. Many are called, but few are chosen, I am not asking you, I'm telling you that you have been handpicked and you will do it."

They say God is a gentleman, but I disagree because he just "gangstered" me into position. It was his way or the highway to hell. I mean what do you say to all of that? Nothing, absolutely nothing. I was speechless for days. I couldn't believe I insulted the Lord like that, especially after making a vow to him that I'd live for him if he'd saved my life. I felt so bad and ashamed. I didn't even want to pray because I didn't feel worthy to speak to him. What was I going to say? "Umm, my bad Jesus". Another reason why I was speechless was because what and how was I going to tell people that the Lord has ordained me just a year and a half after leaving the porn industry? Yes, I was a born-again Christian who loved the Lord and wanted to live for him wholeheartedly, but people didn't see that. They saw a girl who used to drop it like it's hot all over town.

Not only did my past flaws and failures affect me, but my current battle was a hinderance too. At that time, I was able to clean up my foul language, but I didn't really like people and I think that is a requirement, so how was I going to interact and minister to them? I still had the "Compton demon" aka a bust you in your head spirit that wasn't trying to loose me anytime soon. I had no tolerance for disrespect, and I knew a whole lot of it would come my way because of my past. I knew no one in the church would accept me and there was a mental battle of acceptance and fear of being judged that was holding me hostage. It wasn't just an issue of being accepted by others, but mainly learning to accept myself and the previous decisions I made. It had only been a year and a half since I got out the game before all this ministry stuff came about, so the shame, guilt and embarrassment were still fresh. I couldn't even say the word prostitute because I was so ashamed to admit that I was one, as if escort sounded any better. The question was raised again, "why me?"

In the mist of my pity party, the Holy Ghost checked me again. "Are you done yet? Are you done worrying about people who don't have a Heaven or Hell to put you in? You don't have to justify or clarify anything to anybody. I AM God, the only one you must answer to. Did the people you're so worried about hang on a cross and die for you? Was it them that covered you, protected you or called you? The time has come for you to stop worrying about the opinions of people and do what I told you to do." Once again, I was speechless, but not for long.

I started thinking about how even in an unworthy state, God kept me and covered me. I thought about the drugs that I should've overdosed on. I thought about my mind and how I didn't lose it after being molested and raped not just at the age of eight and twelve, but even in the streets while "working", I was constantly attacked. I thought about condoms that broke when I laid with strangers and how I never caught an STD from any of them. I thought about situations I was in and that if it had not been for the Lord on my side, I would have died an early death or been in prison for the rest of my life. I thought about how I was in sin, but when I called on the name of Jesus, he showed up for me time and time again. I came into the realization that I owe no man nothing, but I owe God everything. If he wanted me to testify, I was going to testify. If he wanted me to preach, I was going to preach. If he wanted me to write books, I was going to write books. In the midst of me still saying "why me?" The Lord said, "why not you?! Through your story I can get the Glory and many people can be set free from your truth. You've been through so much and you can touch a host of people from all walks of life. If they see that you can be saved, they will know they can be saved, delivered and healed too. I have need of you."

Ladies and gentlemen, that is the moment when I got delivered from the unwanted thoughts and

Preaching In Pain

opinions of people and boldly accepted the call on my life to minister the Gospel. Too bad no one else accepted it.

Chapter 2- No Support!

From the time I was twelve to twenty, I was a disappointment to my family. I even received the title "The Worst" from my friends because I was in fact a hot mess. They never knew that my behavior resulted from molestation, rape and the aftereffects of my father trying to kill me as a child, they just thought I was crazy. However, I never justified my lifestyle or actions. I knew I had severe issues, so, it was beyond a happy moment for me when I finally got delivered from my past and present demons and changed my life. I made the mistake in believing everyone would celebrate and share that same happiness with me as well, which they did, temporarily.

Preaching In Pain

The fact that I gave my life to Christ was a relief to many. I guess they figured now I'd stop raising so much hell. They congratulated me and told me constantly how proud they were of me that I changed my life for the better. I gave up drugs, alcohol, fornication, forgave myself, ditched the thugs I was dating and got rid of the mean spirit. Deliverance was painful, but necessary and I conquered it. I had many in my corner when I was just a born-again Christian sitting in the pews, but as soon as I announced that God called me to ministry things quickly changed.

The same people who congratulated and supported me were now insulting me. I guess me being a Christian was acceptable, but me being a Minister of the Gospel was taking it a little too far. The support started to diminish as they laughed at me, mocked me and down talked me; but that's what I get for thinking I could maintain my friendships with strippers and porn stars. I should have known they wouldn't understand. However, the most disheartening part was the lack of support from Christians. My past blinded them and although they fake praised God for my testimony, it was still too raunchy for a Minister. No support from my worldly friends and no support from the church people didn't stop me, I was going to do what God called me to do by any means necessary even if I had to do it alone.

I was working a "9 to 5" while developing my ministry, but the more I clocked in, the more discomfort I felt. I knew God was calling me to full time ministry as the ministry invitations quickly multiplied. Not that I was surprised, but my testimony became high in demand and my ministry engagements began to increase and conflict with my work schedule. I tried to ignore doing ministry full time and just find ways to fit it in with my job, fearing that people would really think I was crazy if I quit. Who leaves a decent paying job for the unknown? Somebody crazy, that's who. Ministry wasn't paying me nearly what this job was offering or even what the current job I had at the time. Quite frankly, some things may sound crazy to you and other people, but God's ways are not our ways and even though I couldn't make sense of it I felt him pulling. The real test was when I finally got the call to a career I'd dreamed about. Before, during and after the porn industry, I always had a desire to be a 911 dispatcher for LAPD. I never thought it would happen, but I filled out the application anyway. I kind of forgot about it as ministry and the other job consumed my time, and then I got the email for the interview. I was ecstatic! I was preparing for the interview when I saw it was on the same day that I was supposed to go minister internationally for the first time. I had a choice to make, it was ministry or my dream career. A guaranteed paycheck or live by faith? My ticket to go to the Islands was already booked and my interview for the job was already scheduled. Whatever choice I would've made would have altered my life from that point forward.

It was hard, but I chose ministry over a career. Knowing and understanding that we walk by faith and not by sight, I couldn't worry about how, who or what, I had to trust God. I made a vow in that basement when I told him if he let me live, I'd change my life for him; that meant whatever he said I would do, even if it made me look foolish. No one was there with me when I was running from bullets and locked up in some crazy man's basement, so I didn't have to answer to man. I put in my two weeks' notice and prepared myself for full time ministry. When I made the announcement that I quit my job so I could fulfill my spiritual assignment, the true colors and opinions of those around me started to come out.

My family made sure to tell me every chance they got that I was making a big mistake. They said that was the dumbest decision I've ever made, I could've sworn stripping and doing porn may have been dumber, but hey. They said since I chose to quit, I was not able to come to them for a dime. They did not offer financial or moral support me in any kind of way and they constantly bashed my choices. My father has been a "popcorn" dad since I was twelve years old; he would pop up every now and then, so when he happened to be around this particular time his advice was, "preach later, work now." I had no support and I felt alone. Here I am thinking they would be elated that I made such a drastic turn around and I was on fire for the Lord, but it was the complete opposite. Don't get me wrong, they loved the fact that I changed, and I was so passionate about Christ, but they felt I could do the church thing and still have a career. I was made to feel like I was doing something wrong, I even questioned was it really God that I heard or my own voice. Lord knows I would have much rather had a long lasting, high paying, career in the police department over dodging darts from the devil on a full-time basis.

I tried my hardest to ignore the lack of support, but truth is I couldn't. If your own family isn't rooting for you then who do you turn to? I later found out that blood ain't always thicker than water and sometimes strangers support you better than your relatives. Constantly being told that my ministry move was a mistake, my confidence level began to drop, and I started to question the call again. The Lord quickly assured me that it was his voice and as my calendar started filling up, it was my confirmation that I couldn't do this and have an outside work schedule. I often asked my family, (with an attitude) how can you not support an act of God? Being a Minister of the Gospel is one of the hardest yet best job you can have. Maybe deep down, they just didn't feel I was fit for the position. People, especially family, will often identify you by your mistakes and even though they see the transformation they are still reminded of the old you. I know my family loves me, but I don't think they know the impact of their words and how it was weighing me down.

I was overwhelmed with negativity. My worldly friends were negative, church folks were negative, my testimony had gone viral and even some of the strangers in the comments were negative and my family was negative. It was becoming depressing. At times, before I would get up to speak, their negative words and criticisms would replay in the back of my mind. There were many days that I would fill out applications and was going to go back to work to shut the mouths of my family members. I tried to be a people pleaser when I knew what God had called me to do. I found myself working part time jobs here and there just to keep the peace and show that my decision to go into ministry full time was not an excuse to be lazy, as a matter of fact it wasn't even my decision in the first place. To be honest, I would have picked the career over this, but I know what God told me. I was just being disobedient and defying what I knew, in order to please them. I tried to look at it from their point of view. I was twenty-one years old living on my own and paying my own bills, how was ministry going to support my basic necessities? Truth be told, I didn't even have the answer because I really didn't know, my only defense was that God was going to take care of my business while I took care of his business. One thing I never did was let them see me sweat, even though I was scared I let my faith speak for me because I was confident in God, but they just gave me a look of confusion and irritation. All they heard was blah, blah, no job, blah, blah, full time ministry, blah, blah, no money.

I took that into consideration, but that's not the plan God had for me. I couldn't get a job anyway because I was in and out of town constantly doing ministry and I loved it. As far as I was concerned, ministry was my job, did it give me a lavish lifestyle? Not at all, but it was enough to make ends meet and it fulfilled my soul. Some people love going to work every day and so did I because ministry is a job, period. Without the support of my family, I continued to do what the Lord told me to do; my faith was all the support I needed.

Chapter 3- Church Folks

I'm from the streets and I didn't have much experience with leaders outside of the ones who paid me for sex; nor did I have any experience in being involved with church and ministry or knowing how messy it can really get. Yes, my grandparents kept me in the Baptist church as a child, I even sang in the youth choir and got turned out to prostitution by my choir member, but I still didn't know church folks like that. Yes, I went to many church services whenever I wasn't too hungover on Sunday morning's and would see some of my clients sitting on the front row with their families like they didn't just pay me to fulfill their sick fantasies the night before, but I still didn't know church folks like that. Just like most worldly people, your idea of Christians is that they live up to a certain standard; they are loving, prayerful, kind and always showing the grace of God. From a worldly sinner's perspective, you believe that the church folks will welcome you into the city of refuge with open arms and praise God for your deliverance and your urge to want to be saved. SIKE! Unfortunately, that is not the case and I found out quickly.

When I first came into the church after leaving the industry, I came looking like my sin; a hoe to be exact, which is what I was. I looked like one, I dressed like one, I walked like one, I even smelled like one as I was drenched in the cheap, but loud Bath & Body spray. They said come as you are, and that's what I did, but my goal was not to stay like that. I tried to understand the push back from the saints, but even in that I still should have been welcomed as a sinner saved by grace. That wasn't the case though, which was fine because I was so hungry for God that their stares, frowns and gossip didn't detour me. I was persistent in getting my deliverance and healing, because my life counted on it, this was personal. I was able to withstand the early introduction of church folks, however, I had no clue how terrible they could really be until I got involved in ministry.

I got licensed April 8th, 2010 and immediately began getting invited to different churches, high schools, universities, radio and television shows both nationally and internationally. Don't get me wrong I was overjoyed for a moment, but my excitement quickly drifted as I was shocked and appalled at the response from these self-proclaimed Bible believers. I had some negative commentary from the outside world as they loved to quote the nonsense of "Once a hoe, always a hoe" and "You can't turn a hoe into a housewife", on top of the "This is temporary, she'll be back". I heard that so much until it became laughable. I developed tough skin from the insults of worldly people because as the Bible states in **1 Corinthians 2:14**, but the natural man does not receive the things of the Spirit of God, for they are foolishness to him; nor can he know them, because they are spiritually discerned. It was in my understanding that they just didn't get it and I was ok with that, but what I wasn't ok with was the response from the church folks. I was flabbergasted by the judgment, hate and mistreatment from them because of my testimony. Are they not reading the same Bible I'm reading? Are they not serving the same God I'm serving? Am I missing something here? These are the same people who are praising God about David who committed murder and adultery, the same people who are running around the church about Paul who hated Christians and persecuted the church, these same people are shouting about the woman at the well who was obviously a part of the same game I was with her having five husbands and shacking with a sixth man. Am I not like the people you're praising God about? I couldn't understand how you can be thankful for the testimony of people you've never seen but reject mine. The Bible says in **1 John 4:20**, If someone says, "I love God," and hates his brother, he is liar, for he does not love his brother whom he has seen, how can he love God whom he has not seen? How do you love David, Paul and the rest who have fallen to sin whom you've never encountered, and yet hate me while I'm standing right here in your face?

They were bold with it too. I remember I was booked to go to the Caribbean and the church that was hosting me was promoting the event on the radio. I remember the radio host was not aware that I'd be on the call and he stated that "a person like me shouldn't even be welcomed into their country." This was a Gospel station, and the host was a leader in his church. I was floored, but unstoppable and still a little hood, so I made sure that I was taken to that radio station when I got there. Let's just say the host had a different tone when I pulled up.

As my story was gaining more attention, people were excited to tell their Pastor's about me in hopes of getting me to minister to the youth and young adults at their churches. When I would follow up, in a disappointed tone they would tell me that their Pastor's said they didn't want me in their pulpits. My first book had just come out and I actually asked a very well-known Evangelist in the L.A area if I could sell my books at her conference since she advertised vendor spaces. She looked at me and said, "Girl, don't you know this is a godly conference?" She then laughed and walked away. A godly conference? As if my story wasn't godly. I guess she only heard the porn part and ignored the rest; or maybe she didn't view me as "godly".

That was just the beginning of my battles with church folks which continued to get even more disheartening. I later found out that my testimony was so exciting to some for many different reasons and a lot of the invites weren't coming because they wanted to hear a message of deliverance. I was getting invited by a lot of male Pastors and soon found out that the invite wasn't just to the church. I remember speaking to a Pastor who was getting my information to book my flight and during the conversation he mentioned that I was his favorite porn-star and he was looking forward to the fellowship. The Holy Ghost in me stopped me from cussing him out and I immediately hung up to prevent a potential rape.

I realized that my testimony exposes the hidden things. It'll either expose the true character of a so-called believer and ignite their judgmental spirit, or it will expose the hidden lust and perversions of a leader as well as others. I learned quickly not to look for acceptance from those within the four walls because it wasn't in there. I was treated like a joke, from pew members as well, as they watched my movies while I was up ministering; yep, you read that right. I have been up ministering the Gospel and people were viewing my movies at the same time. Even the people in position, which I expected so much more from engaged. Although it was hurtful, I didn't use "church hurt" as a poor excuse to end my relationship with God. People can be cruel, but it wasn't people who saved me. A man, woman, boy or girl should not and does not have the power to dictate your walk with God, so they were going to have to come at me harder than that…..and they did.

Preaching In Pain

Not only having to deal with the rejection of church folks, I also had to be guarded because I never knew the motive. It was like they either shunned me or tried to pull me in closely. I do know that everyone was not out to get me so there were a few leaders who I felt comfortable with. I got a call from a Pastor who was familiar with my story and offered to mentor me. We setup a day to go to lunch so he could give me some ministerial tools and books. He picked me up because I didn't have a car at the time and again, he knew my story and I was familiar with him and his wife. We went to lunch and everything was awesome, no weird vibes or flirtation of any kind. After our meal and hours of church talk, we headed back to my home. Before I exited the vehicle, the Pastor asked me to pray and I was more than willing. As I bowed my head and closed my eyes to engage in prayer, I was startled when the man of God grabbed my face and put his tongue in my mouth! He looked shocked at my disinterest. I quickly opened the door and walked swiftly into my house. Nothing surprised me because I don't put nothing past anyone, but in that moment, I was puzzled. Who the heck tongue kisses someone in the middle of prayer! You would think that buddy would've gotten the picture by my response to his unwanted lips, but nope. He kept calling and texting me, feening for an affair, need I remind you that I knew his wife, she happened to be the Evangelist that laughed in my face and told me I couldn't sell my books at her godly conference. The fleshly side of me could've ran with this, but that wasn't who I was anymore, and I kept having to prove that. When he finally realized that I had no intentions or interest in being his side chick, the Preacher man asked if he could be my sugar daddy. As if the money offer would make me say yes. What Mr. Man did not know was the fastest way to turn me off is to treat me like a prostitute. I literally put in blood, sweat and tears to hold on to my deliverance and I be doggone if I'd let someone treat me as if I was still in that place! I've never been a snitch, so I kept his little secret safe until he pissed me off with his prostitution proposition. (yes, if you have a sugar daddy, you're a prostitute.) I threatened to tell his wife if he didn't leave me alone, I may have also said a few choice words as well.

I had not been exposed to what happens beyond Sunday morning service until I got licensed and ordained. I saw another side of church folk, the ones in the pulpit and in the pews. Thankfully, I've never been a weak woman, so I didn't allow the foolishness from the people to take me off my assignment. With no real support system within Christendom, I kept going.

Chapter 4-Where Is Jehovah-Jireh?

A year had passed since I quit my job and went into full time ministry and I must say finances definitely changed. When I first began, my ministry assignments were often, I was on the road more than I was home and assignments, appearances and book sales brought in enough funds. It was enough to cover rent and household bills as well as ministry expenses, but before I knew it things drastically changed. The invites were no longer coming in every week, they started coming in once a month and then every other month. Was my fifteen minutes of fame over? Was I no longer a needed voice? Weeks went by and I'd be sitting at home trying to keep the faith because I know God said full time, but there's no food in the fridge. I was believing God, but I had no money to buy more products for my ministry. The Bible states in **2 Corinthians 5:7,** For we walk by faith, not by sight, but my rent was due. I remember rapid weight loss and when people started to notice my small frame, I just said that I was fasting. That sounded better than saying I was poor, but that was the reality. I wasn't fasting, I was starving. One day I opened my refrigerator and there was just an expired milk carton and one bottle of water. I was very self-conscience and paranoid when I went to church hoping people wouldn't notice that I was wearing the same outfit from two Sunday's ago because I couldn't afford to buy new clothes to fit my new size. I didn't ask my family for assistance because they already made it clear that they would not help me in anyway. I was grateful yet ashamed when my best friend Pierra gave me her clothes and shoes to wear just so I can have something. I would often turn down invites to go to restaurants so I wouldn't embarrass myself

myself when the check came. I knew people would pay for my meal, but I never wanted to be a burden to anyone. Pierra would pick me up on her lunch breaks; her job was near my house and her and her mom would make sure I ate that day. She was my best friend and never once made me feel bad about her kind gestures, but I started to feel like a charity case, so I stopped telling her that I didn't have food. I just went without for a few days at a time. The hunger pains started to pierce me, and I found myself going on dates with multiple guys just so I can eat. No sex, just wasted time; sorry, but I was hungry.

The ministry engagements didn't completely stop, but not all of them had love offerings attached to them. Money has never and will never be my motive for ministry, so I would still accept certain invites even if it didn't have an honorarium attached to it. Most television and radio interviews don't come with a check, so I was on TV looking pretty with my best friend's dress on talking about how good God is, when in fact I had a major attitude with him. Yes, I was angry with God; I submitted to his instructions, and this is the end result? I'm walking around here talking about faith, but truth be told, I was a little confused and upset with mine.

It was becoming unbearable so I had to get a job doing something, I would babysit a few times a week, but it still wasn't enough. It allowed me to live off of milk and cereal from Superior Market and keep my cell phone on. I was being flown first class and put in lavish, five-star hotels, while having to go back home to a garage. Yes, I lived in a garage for years, in Inglewood, CA. A nice Jamaican lady, who became like family to me, converted her garage into a studio. It had carpet, a small closet and bathroom, enough space for a full-size bed, a refrigerator and a broken television. I don't know if she felt sorry for me or if it was because we both were of Jamaican descent, but she helped me as much as she could. She knew I had no money and would offer me a bowl of bully beef or oxtails with rice & peas for dinner. I was months behind on rent and she never put me out.

Whole time I was angry at God because I knew

he said full time ministry and I obeyed just to end up in this situation, but he was still providing, just not in the way I had expected it. He used my best friend to provide clothes and food, he used my landlord to provide a roof over my head, he allowed my church family to provide their transportation, so I get back and forth to service. I felt like a charity case, I was embarrassed and felt less than, but he was still making provisions. This was extremely hard for someone who went from independence and having a lavish worldly lifestyle to being here in this humbled place. In **1 Kings 17:5-6,** it talks about God sending the Ravens to feed the Prophet Elijah. Often times, we expect God to move one way and he does it another way and it may cause confusion and even upset your spirit, but in the end, he is still making a way, it's just not your way. So, I tried to keep hope alive and stay positive during what I called my wilderness season.

Things got bad as I continued to live in this garage, drop weight from not properly eating, being car-less and catching the bus, but I stayed faithful to my assignment and things started to slowly turn around. The invites started coming in again and I began getting invited to more churches and events meeting more people in ministry. Of course, I thought this was a great thing, until I found out what those meetings would become.

Chapter 5: Love, Lust & Infatuation

My last relationship, if that's what you want to call it, ended in 2009 and I decided to practice celibacy. After years of stripping, prostitution and pornography, my body deserved a break; plus, I was more focused on living my life according to God's principles. I had no desire for sex or a relationship of any sort. I needed healing and deliverance not more soul ties. My idea of marriage wasn't so great either because most of my clients were married men which led me to believe all men cheat with prostitutes, and if we were going to discuss marriage, I was already married to my ministry. I consumed myself with doing Kingdom work and although there were some bumps in the road I was still on fire for the Lord. Being with a man or woman romantically didn't even cross my mind...at first.

After almost two years of celibacy I found out that Holiness doesn't put the fire out and that itch came back. Not necessarily for sex, but for companionship and intimacy. Being single wasn't as easy as most people portray it to be unless you're unattractive and not appealing. Now I may not be Beyoncé fine, but a sista' is not so bad on the eye if I must say so myself, and men made that very clear. Most days I felt like a pork chop being chased by dogs, but I wasn't interested in a quickie. I was a stripper and an escort most of my life, so I had many encounters with men, but I'd never been in love with one before. I never even experienced a healthy, loving and faithful relationship and I was starting to desire that. I believe God was softening me up, my hardcore stance on men and marriage began to dwindle and I couldn't believe that I fixed my mouth to say I wanted to be married. Yes, me the ex-porn star who hated men and viewed them as lying, weird fetish having freaks, now wanted a husband. I must admit, my reasons for wanting to enter marriage may not have been correct at the time. I personally believed that every Minister should be married, I may be wrong, but I just don't trust a single Preacher. Plus, I was so ministry driven that I wanted my marriage to be a part of my ministry. I figured being married is another avenue to glorify God, while glorifying my needs too. I thought being married would subdue the temptation of being on the road all the time. It can be distracting to meet so many attractive people who share so many similarities with you and not be tempted to have a need met. So basically, I wanted to get married so I can have sex legally and we can serve the Lord together. Another reason was because I had a chip on my shoulder and a point to prove. I was constantly told that no man would marry me because of my past which I thought was ludicrous because I had to beat the men away. However, I started to realize that there is a difference between a man sleeping with you, vs a man marrying you. Sure, I can pull them in by the dozens to hit it and quit it, but could I be chosen as a wife was the real question. Again, after constantly being told that a man would never marry me, I wanted to shut them up. I was going to have the last laugh.

If I'd be honest, I didn't just want to prove the naysayers wrong, but I wanted to prove something to myself as well. The mistakes of my past were a secret insecurity for me and quiet as kept I felt the same way they did. I questioned if a man would really choose me as a wife and mother to his children knowing the life I once lived. It was evident that I had become a changed woman, but would a real man be comfortable and secure in knowing his lovely wife was involved in the sex industry? Those questions crossed my mind daily, driving me crazy and fueling my fire to want to marry for all the wrong reasons, so the dating began.

It started off nice because this was new; I wasn't messing with the typical drug dealing, pimping thugs that I was used to, but I was meeting nice men with careers and some act right. Like a fool, I thought every guy I met was "the one." I remember I met this broker named "Jeff"; he was the total opposite of me. He was a blue-collar guy that worked in a downtown high rise, with no tattoos, he had a home in the suburbs and one daughter. For once, I didn't have to hide my past like I did with previous men. I was too ashamed to tell them that I worked in the sex industry, but of course they'd end up finding out and when they did things took a turn. They went from being gentlemen to wanting to instantly have sex with me or they would run like the wind, which discouraged me from dating altogether. However, Jeff was different and although it was difficult to be honest about my experiences, it was necessary if I was going to move forward with someone, so I told him the truth, expecting him to give me a goodbye, but to my surprise, he didn't want to jump my bones on the spot, nor did he run away. He simply responded with a "we all make mistakes and choices in life, some we're not so proud of, but they make us who we are." I was floored and turned on at the same time. I couldn't believe it because I'd never gotten that response before from a man. I just knew we were going to get married. We continued to see each other, he introduced me to his sister and his daughter which they both were so sweet to me, he would leave me the keys to his home and he never once asked me for sex or made me uncomfortable in anyway. This seemed just too good to be true....and it was.

Jeff was absolutely amazing in most areas, but where we clashed was on our religious beliefs. I was a diehard Christian and absolutely lived my life according to Biblical principles. I wanted my man to have the same beliefs. The Bible says in **1 Corinthians 11:3,** But I want you know that the head of every man is Christ, the head of woman is man, and the head of Christ is God. In order for a man to lead me he has to follow Christ, but that wasn't going to happen with Jeff. He was an active Jehovah's Witness, and he had no plans on conforming and neither did I. His work around for us was to just not talk about religion and I can continue to do my Christian thing while he does his Jehovah Witness thing, and everything will be great, but that didn't work for me. In fact, it was deal breaker. **2 Corinthians 6:14** says, do not be unequally yoked together with unbelievers. It was hard to let him go because this man was dang near perfect, he had money, he was attractive, he was an excellent father with no baby mama drama, he was the perfect gentleman to me, but that one thing was a big thing and I just couldn't continue on in a relationship with a man who refused to serve my God, so my fairytale romance ended. Jeff and I weren't together long enough for me to be super heartbroken, but I was sad at our split.

Not long after, I ended up reverting back to what I knew which was thug love. It wasn't on purpose this time either, he was just a familiar face. His name was "Tee", I used to mess with his uncle back in the day. His uncle was a pimp that taught me a lot about the game, but we obviously had no more dealings when I turned "square." Tee had a tattoo shop which he sold hair out of, amongst other things. I needed some bundles, so I went to him to get them. He was tall, thin, attractive with long, beautiful hair. I never paid attention to him when I was with his uncle because we both would have been shot, so this was the first time I actually noticed him. He flirted, I flirted back, he asked for my number and I gave it to him; Lord why did I do that. We talked every day and saw each other often, but we both treaded lightly because I was a Minister and he was a drug dealing, tattoo artist. However, as much as we tried to ignore our intense attraction for one another, we eventually fell hard.

I was with this man all the time, he would never go to church with me, but he'd wait for me to get out so he could pick me up. Unlike Jeff, he didn't refuse to be a Christian, he just didn't live like one at the moment. I knew his lifestyle wasn't the best for where I was going, but what I was drawn to was the fact that he tried to be and do better when I was around. Tee would spray a deadly amount of cologne to get the weed smell out of his car and house so I wouldn't rebuke him. I thought this might last, after all the Bible does say a in **1 Corinthians 7:14,** for the unbelieving husband is sanctified by the wife, and I was going to ride that all the way out. Too bad I couldn't.

Tee and I were getting ready to go out on a date that evening. I was getting dressed when my phone rang. He was on the line, but he didn't sound like himself. First thing I thought was that the police got him, I was never prepared for what he was about to say. With his voice trembling, he said, "While I was in the shower, I felt the presence of God so strongly that I had to get out of the shower and lay prostrate on my bathroom floor. I felt him so strong, all I could do was cry. Danielle, God spoke to me and said, leave her alone, she doesn't belong to you, she's mine. I don't know who you are, but you're special to God. I promise I didn't have bad intentions for you, but I can't have you. Please don't ever call me again, I can't see you anymore." He hung up the phone and just like that it was over. I didn't even try to call him back because I was in a state of shock too. I mean Tee was a street dude and for God to reveal himself to him like that wasn't just scary for him, but for me too. Some may say

I had no business with him in the first place, but he treated me better than the "men of God" I met and to be honest I was annoyed that God didn't let me have him.

I laid low for a while not looking for anything to jump into. I was going to a mega church in Compton for a while and there he was. A reformed gangster who found the Lord while on lockdown. He was now one of the Pastors' at the church that I was attending, and someone made the introduction because of our similar past. After hearing my testimony, he asked if I'd be interested in speaking to some ex-convicts and without hesitation I accepted. When I arrived at the location the following day, I met with the group, shared my testimony and it was an awesome turn out. As I was leaving, I was stopped by Pastor "Joey". He asked if I could stay a few more minutes and I didn't see any problem with that, so I stayed. When the meeting was over, he walked me to my car and told me how great my interaction was with the people and blah, blah, blah, then he asked me on a date. Now,

Pastor Joey was fine! He was just my type too, buff, a little hood, but educated, sophisticated and saved. I said "Yeah, sure we can go out." We exchanged phone numbers and talked almost every day. Unlike with Jeff, I didn't want to see Joey every day. I knew there'd be some sexing and fornication going on if we did. Our chemistry and sexual tension were high. He wasn't quiet about it either, so we kept our distance, but would still talk and see each other in public places. Joey asked me to spend the weekend in Big Bear with him, lying about how we wasn't going to do anything but spend quality time. In my mind, I was like negro please! I knew there would be some butt naked sex going on and us being alone for the weekend in a romantic cabin probably wasn't the best idea, but I said yes anyway. I figured even if we did "fall" we were going to get married. We talked about marriage often and we fit like a glove. He was an ex-thug and I was an ex-everything. He was saved and working with ex-cons. I was saved and working with strippers and prostitutes. He was in ministry. I was in ministry and we both were very attracted to one another. I saw this as a long-term thing and I wanted him because he too, accepted me for me knowing where I came from. There were no secrets and I just knew this would have a happy ending. Boy was I wrong!

The church that he and I attended had three services. Since I'm not an early morning person, I would normally attend the 11am and/or 6pm service and Joey was aware of that. We had to push our Big Bear trip back due to our schedules which was a good thing because we both knew there wouldn't be any Bible study going on that weekend. I happen to be up extra early one Sunday morning and decided to go to the 8am service. I never do early services, but that day I just so happen to. I got to church, everything went according to program and then Pastor Joey takes the mic. He greeted the church and before he began his wonderful speech, he introduced his whole wife and two daughters to the congregation! They stood up and I almost fell down. Your wife!? At what point were you going to inform me of a wife and some children sir Pastor? I was numb. The old me would've tore

Preaching In Pain

the church up and got banned for life, but the new me sat there, numb and speechless. I couldn't move, I couldn't focus, did this negro just introduce his whole wife? You couldn't pay me to tell you what the sermon was that day because I didn't hear anything past, "my lovely wife and daughters." When service was over, I walked super-fast to my car, cussing him out in my head. Now, I've had my share of married liars, but not from a Pastor! I was and still am one of the ones who actually hold Ministers to a certain standard. Yes, we are human however that is not an excuse to live foul. I drove home and laid down because at that point I had a headache. Around 1pm, this man called me like nothing happened. "Hey, I was looking for you at 11 o'clock service today, I didn't see you." I said, "Yeah, because I was at 8am service." He goes silent. "Lovely family. Funny how they were never mentioned." He's still silent. I began to cuss him out from here to Wakanda. He finally speaks and says, "I'm sorry, but it's not what it looks like." "Bleep! It looks like you got a whole wife sir!" He goes silent. "Pastor, you have a great day. Goodbye." Crack is what it was, it had to be crack for this man to tell me a whole family isn't what it looks like. I was hurt, but more than anything I was angry and just like that my potential marriage ministry dream was over.

I was so disturbed as if I had learned nothing from the streets. I have seen just about everything and have experienced every kind of man and every kind of lie they can tell, but this hit different. We are Ministers, we're in the church, where is the standard? How did you preach the Gospel and exhort people while living a double life? I was appalled and dumbfounded. Maybe I expected too much out of a man with a title, but then again, I should! He's a freaking Preacher for crying out loud. I was done again. To me all men were the same, church men or street men, it didn't make a difference. I refocused my attention solely on ministry and not marriage and got back to work…and boom! There he was.

I didn't leave the mega church completely after Pastor Joey and I split. I did, however, visit other churches in hopes of fellowshipping somewhere

Preaching In Pain

else permanently. After being gone for some time, I was invited back to share my testimony once again at the youth conference. I was ecstatic too because the main speaker was my favorite Pastor. I had watched him on *TBN* and *The Word Network* for some time, what caught my attention was how he titled his sermons. They were very catchy, and you couldn't help but to listen to what he had to say. When his segment was over, I ran to YouTube to look him up. I was being drawn in more and more as I watched multiple preaching videos and interviews of him almost every day. He was a big time Preacher of a mega church on the East Coast and he had a whole lot of swag. I didn't know much about his personal life; all I knew is this black man was on TV and preaching to my soul. He unknowingly enlightened and empowered me as a young and upcoming Minister, and I admired him deeply.

After he heard my testimony at the service that night, he asked for my contact information and I had to play as if I wasn't star struck. I slid him my business card and gave him my book *From Porn To The Pulpit.* I didn't know what he was going to do with my number. I just thought he was being nice and was going to toss it in the trash the moment he walked out of the door, so I asked for a picture like a fan and didn't think anything more about it. The next morning my phone rang, and I saw his name on the caller ID! I almost fell out of bed as I jumped up and cleared my man sounding morning voice. "Hello!" I answered so frantically. He told me that he stayed up all night reading my book, he couldn't put it down and he was so proud of me. He invited me to share my testimony and speak to the youth at his church and although I was in a state of shock I was honored and said absolutely. I couldn't believe my favorite Pastor whom I watched on television for years invited me to speak on his major platform. The date was set, and I was flown first class and put in a five-star hotel, just super giggly, excited and in a state of disbelief. Once I mounted the platform to share my testimony, God moved, and people were set free. We had some good ole church that day and I thought that's where it started and ended between him and I, but we hadn't even begun.

A few weeks later, he called me again. He was in

Preaching In Pain

L.A preaching at a church not too far from my house and invited me to come out. Without hesitation, I got dressed and headed out to see the man of God, I wasn't going to miss seeing my favorite Preacher, especially on a personal invite. That man knows he can preach, and he tore the church up, per usual. Shortly after it was over, I tried to greet him in the lobby, but because of his celebrity status he was surrounded by many, so I just waved and headed home. I got to my front door, looked at my phone and saw two missed calls and a text from the Preacher man. The text read, "Hey, why did you leave? How far are you? Can you come back? I quickly responded and said, "Of course! I'm on my way back now." Call me gullible, but I honestly thought that he wanted to introduce me to the Pastor of the church he just preached at. I was new to ministry and assumed he wanted to make a connection for me, but the address he told me to come to wasn't to the church, not even to a restaurant; the address led me to a hotel. I sat in the parking lot trying to convince myself that this was not and could not be a booty call. He read my book so he knew what I had been through and he wouldn't do that to me. Not to mention, he just finished preaching, this is definitely not a booty call.

Still being gullible and naïve, I said maybe everyone is just meeting in the hotel's lounge, but there was no one in the lounge. I gave him a call from the lobby and said, "Hey! I'm here." He said, "Ok, come up to room 1417." I could hear my heartbeat louder and louder as the elevator went up to the fourteenth floor. I didn't know why the Pastor wanted me to come into his hotel room, but I was glad to be in his company. I assumed that all the Ministers were just hanging out in his room or maybe he would suggest mentoring me since I was still a babe in ministry. Whatever I thought was going to happen, was definitely not anything close. I knocked on his door and my innocent smile slowly slid off my face as the shock took over when he opened the door. The man of God was in his drawls! My legs felt like bricks because I couldn't move them. I must've stood there too long because he asked was I going to come in. "Danielle run to the elevator, run now!" I said in my head, and yet my feet took me inside the room.

I walked into the big, extravagant hotel room; it was empty, so the story of the Preachers hanging out went out the window. I nervously sat on the couch and everything seemed to be in slow motion. He flopped on the big king size bed which opened his robe up a little more, exposing his hairy body. I'm staring and not trying to look all at the same time. He said, "Why are you so far away? Come over here." Lord my hands were sweating, and my heart was beating fast as I sat on the bed just a few feet away from the half-naked Preacher that I admired. For the first time ever, I was speechless. Not just because of this awkward position but being around him was intimidating. He was a mega Televangelist that I had been following for some time. "Why are you so quiet?" I really didn't know what to say, so I just started mumbling about how he was my favorite Preacher and how I watched him on TV every day. I started talking about all these other big named, celebrity Pastors and leaders who happened to be his friends, but he wasn't interested in church talk. He engaged in that conversation for a few minutes, but he quickly changed the subject and asked me if I liked him. Of course, I liked him...as a Pastor. I liked watching him on TV because he had a lot of personality and his sermons were so relatable for me as a young adult. He was definitely my fav, so I responded back, "Of course I do!" He went silent, looked at me and said, "prove it."

It's like I forgot everything I learned in the streets, I guess that's because I was no longer a street chick and I didn't view him in that way, so in my mind I asked myself prove it how? What does he want me to do? Gullible, naïve and ignorant I know, but I honestly didn't come here for this. The next thing I know, we were kissing. I was in disbelief, yet in total euphoria because I was having an intimate moment with a man I idolized. He encouraged and inspired me from afar for years and now he's on top of me. The TV went off and so did our clothes. He asked me if I had a condom. I said to myself, "Um excuse me sir, what!? Do I look like I came here with condoms, we just left a revival! You know the one you just preached at? I didn't know we were about to have butt-naked sex!" That was the quick conversation I had in my head as he waited for my response. I whispered, "No, I don't have any, do you?" He sighed and paused for a few seconds and then he continued to kiss me. I guess he was determined to get what he wanted with or without a condom. Before he penetrated me, I told him that I had been celibate for over a year, aka be gentle fool; and that he was. I became intoxicated by his warm embrace and passion. It felt like love making more than a booty call even if it was a façade. That night, I had sex, with this mega Pastor, twice. My conviction quickly set in and in my head, I said, "Oh Lord, I just humped the Preacher!" He eased my convicted mind and even my spirit as held me tight after we completed our final round of intimacy and we fell asleep in each other's arms.

I was awakened the next morning by a forehead kiss, as I opened my eyes, he was getting ready to leave and head to the next city to preach. He told me I can stay in the room an extra night and order whatever I wanted. I said thank you as he kissed me one more time. I laid in that bed in a state of disbelief and amazement. I knew the act was wrong, but I laid there with my heart smiling. I just knew I was about to become the First Lady. We had to be together after this, right? I mean he's a Preacher, so I know he's not out here just having random sex partners. He had to feel something for me, right? These were the thoughts of the young and dumb Danielle.

I was hoping for a fairytale ending with him. The rich and famous Pastor marries the ex-stripper from the hood and together they build a wonderful life of marriage and ministry. However, things didn't quite go that way. He didn't sweep me off my feet nor did he ever discuss an exclusive relationship let alone marriage, but every time he came to L.A he made sure we were together. He would wine and dine me, but I wondered why we weren't going any further. What's taking him so long to ask me to relocate to the East Coast, shoot my bags were packed and sitting at the door. Why haven't I met his kids and his parents? When am I going to pick out my First Lady chair? When are we going to have some excitement outside of the sheets? Seems like he was just fond of my bedroom antics only. I never thought I'd be this chick; you know the one who thinks she can change the way a man feels about her by making his knees weak. I was starting to catch on to him only wanting a sexual relationship, but I figured if he just gets to know the real me, he'd fall in love. I'm already putting it on him, so all I have to do now is get him to see the real me and not just the inside of my vagina. I was infatuated with him and I was willing to be what he wanted if that meant having him. He had me before he ever touched me. I was already engaged with him spiritually and the moment he penetrated me, our soul tie was no longer just spiritual, but now it was a physical connection. So, I tried to show signs that I was a worthy candidate for marriage. I showed him the saved side of me by praying for him before and after he preached. That didn't work. I showed him my silly personality and constantly cracked jokes to make him laugh. That didn't

Preaching In Pain

work. I didn't constantly sweat him on his whereabouts or pressure him into a relationship. That didn't work. I offered to cook him homemade meals and to clean his mansion. That didn't work. I showed interest and concern in his children, his church, his health, his ideas and his overall well-being and guess what? That still didn't work.

I remember we went to the movies one day and he was walking all fast like he didn't want us to be seen together. First of all, you invited me, now you act like you don't want anyone to see us together in this setting. I could've stayed home darling, so I had a major attitude. Help me understand how you're comfortable at every hotel in Los Angeles being seen with me going to your room, but you want to act a fool at the movies. I knew then that his arrogance was going to have me catch a case eventually, but I still couldn't resist him. He kissed me and my frown turned upside down. But after a year of trying to be his everything, he was only interested in one thing, and that was for me to be his booty buddy.

Preaching In Pain

I wanted him so bad that I tried to give him what he wanted until I just couldn't anymore, because I wasn't that type of woman. I never altered myself for anyone, and this situation-ship had revealed to me that this ain't it.

The icing on the cake was our last encounter. In the middle of our lust making, he became very vulgar dropping "f" bombs, now don't get me wrong I'm all for a little bedroom excitement, but this was going left because he just flat out told me that he wanted me to "f" him forever, and instead of him turning me on, he was turning me off. See, he obviously had it twisted. Yeah, I wanted him and hoped that something would spark between us, but what I was not nor will I ever be is desperate. When he felt comfortable enough to say that to me it was like the light bulb went off and I finally realized that I was nothing more to him than what he read about, an ex-pornstar and I was just fulfilling his sexual fantasies. The fastest way to get rid of me is to treat me like a prostitute, which is what he was doing. Eating at nice restaurants and going back to luxury hotels to screw sounds like a blast from my past, the only difference was he didn't leave the money on the dresser. The Pastor who once spoke life to my spirit is now draining it. I wasn't trying to be holier than thou because I was fornicating with this man, but I still expected him to have a little more respect and to be different from the thugs I was used to dating, but he turned out to be even worse. I also realized that mega, don't mean mighty. He mastered the art of preaching, but he had no power. A real man of God will make mistakes, but they don't practice a life of sin with no conviction. My infatuation for him didn't allow me to see the obvious truth until now, so I kindly put my panties back on, walked out and this foolishness was over, or so I thought.

I was just a babe in ministry, but church folks talk and as time was progressing this man's name kept coming up and not in a good way. Everyone who mentioned him had something negative to say, which mainly consisted of his whore-ish ways. I'm a lot of things, but a snitch I could never be, nor do I kiss and tell, so even though it was tearing me up, I just sat there and listened as if I had no clue about who they were referring to. I was devastated at what I was hearing and even reading about him on the blogs. A baby on the way!? Sleeping with the women in his church? I was under the impression that we were exclusive, only to find out that I was one of many. We may not have been in a full-on relationship, but we weren't supposed to be sleeping with other people which is what he told me. I was only intimate with him, but he had a bus load of women and I was just his L.A chick. I was turned off by the gossip because I knew most of it to be true. I just couldn't believe a man of God of this magnitude could really be out here living a double life. I was no longer interested in being his L.A booty call, so I stopped answering the phone calls and I declined the meet ups when he came to my city, but before I could fully remove myself, I missed my period.

I hesitated for a while, but I knew what a missed period meant. I finally took a pregnancy test and unfortunately it was positive. Here we go I said, but deep down I was hoping that once I told him, he and I would discuss marriage to at least save face for ministry, being that we were about to have a baby and we, more so him at the time were very present in the forefront of the church. He was in Africa preaching when I found out the results, I didn't have the courage to call, so I texted him the news. That man has never called me so fast in his life and he was in a panic. For some reason, I thought that he would be much calmer in this situation being that he's been in quite a few of these scenarios before; allegedly there are multiple secret babies. However, I was hoping that we could discuss doing "the right thing" which was getting married and raising our baby together, because truth be told, I did still care about him and I knew he could love me beyond sex if he would open up to it. If he just gave us a chance, he would've fell in love with all of me and not just my body. I was dreaming and he quickly shut down my fairytale. As soon as I picked up the phone, he said, "What's your bank account information so I can send you the money to get rid of that."

I was speechless, I was shocked, I was disturbed. First of all, I don't do abortions, second this can't be the world's favorite Pastor telling me to abort his baby! I told him we'll talk when he got back to the States, I hung up and cried because I was so hurt. I was celibate and content prior to meeting him, I was brand new to ministry and I fell for a "man of God" and we're not talking about just anybody he was one of the top Preachers of that time and telling me to get rid of his child. Where is God at in that? The sin was the pre-marital sex, but my child shouldn't have to die because of it. How could he finish preaching life to thousands of people while telling me to kill the life inside of me? I'm very street smart, but when I got into church fully and entered ministry, I held Preachers to a higher standard. I expected them to be different from the "street dudes". He really hurt my feelings and depression started to kick in. I'm pregnant, unmarried and in the church, but with all that being said, I knew an abortion was out of the question. If I kept the pimp's baby, I was going to keep the Preachers baby too!

He kept calling and texting me to send the abortion money and I kept dodging him. I had an could even make it to the appointment, I was awakened by a sharp pain in my side with blood protruding down my legs. My sheets were covered in blood and I crawled to my bathroom in agony. I knew what was happening because I had been here three times before, but I was hoping it wasn't an actual miscarriage. I didn't go to the hospital right away as I was trying to convince myself that everything was ok, so I just waited two days later for my appointment. The Pastor continued calling to get my bank information. Since I was fresh out the "game" I played him like he played me. I went ahead and gave him the account number; go ahead and pay me, but I'm still not getting an abortion was my attitude. He put the money in my account and waited on the confirmation that it was done. However, the doctor had confirmed I miscarried for the third time. Till this day he believes I aborted that baby, but in actuality, I went shopping, so if you're reading this, thanks for the hair I bought and the bills I paid with your abortion money buddy.

I spent his money on what I wanted because I

desperately needed a little pick me up, especially since the doctor looked at my medical records and saw two previous miscarriages, now this being my third. I don't think I was able to really grasp the severity of my health situation because I was still very angry with the pimping Preacher and how he mishandled me, so I wasn't processing much at that time. After dealing with him, I was exhausted, drained and done. Being with him reopened wounds that I thought had healed. I was completely turned off and had no desire to date or sleep with anyone else. Not only did I fear pregnancy at this point, I feared another heartbreak. I was just over men and any thoughts of a relationship with them and boom! There SHE was.

It's no secret that I'd been with multiple women since I was twelve. My first encounter happened to be through a guy that I was dating. He had a girlfriend, but instead of her wanting to beat me up for messing with her man, she wanted me for herself. I was a well-developed, fast twelve-year-old at the time and they were fifteen. Let's just say she was well advanced for her age and taught me things that I had no clue about. To be honest, I wasn't super excitement about my first lesbian experience, however, as time went on, I found myself being hurt continually by boys and men which pushed me more to the same sex; molestation and rape will do that to you. It wasn't mainly a sexual thing for me, I just found comfort in being with females because for one I couldn't get pregnant and the experiences weren't as painful as it was when I was with men, so I thought. Truth is, I went through more drama with women than I ever did with men. When I was in the world, all my serious relationships were with females, I just engaged with men for money. Unlike the "God made me this way" generation of LGBTQ folks, I knew it wrong, so when I found myself having same-sex attractions I constantly prayed for God to remove the desire, and he did!

The last girl I was with for several years, slept with my "friend" and after trying to kill both of them, I was done with women for a very long time. Celibacy came for a little while and then I started dating thugs and Preachers, which did nothing but keep me pregnant and heart broken.

Preaching In Pain

I was turned off by men and constantly praying that my pain didn't turn back into perversion, but there she was.

I went to speak at a church, and she was the Pastor's armor bearer. My "gay-dar" quickly went off because you could tell she was in or just coming out of that lifestyle, but even then, there wasn't an instant attraction, just a familiar spirit. I spoke at the church, left and didn't think anything of it. Later that night I received a friend request from her, I accepted and then there was an inbox shortly after. She said, "Hey sis, just wanted to connect with you." I didn't see the harm in that, so we exchanged information. We talked often, I invited her to a church service, the following week she invited me to lunch and from there things seemed to take an unexpected turn. The flirting began, phone conversations got longer, the urge to hang out got stronger and it became an everyday thing. We both were aware of the feelings that were growing, but I refused to admit it or give it any attention. She would flirt and make certain comments, but I continued to turn a blind eye to the obvious, until I couldn't anymore.

One day, she invited me over to "talk" and within five minutes of the conversation she asked if I felt the same way she felt. No longer could I deny it, I said yes. She gazed into my eyes and we exchanged a kiss. Instantly, we both knew that wasn't a good idea, but at this point Pandora's box had been bust wide open as the tension between us was thick. Before she could embrace me again, I jumped in my car and sped away, rebuking myself. "What are you doing!?" Was the constant question I asked myself while speeding down the street. I was a woman of God, she was a woman of God (or so I thought) this can't be happening. "This is bad!" I said, but not just for the obvious reason, but it was bad because I could not shake her at this point. Although feelings had grown, I was in denial of what was really going on. I refused to believe that I had become entangled in lesbianism again. "I'm not gay!" is what I told myself constantly. "I like men! How the heck did this happen!?" I hadn't desired a woman, nor did I have any sexual attraction towards them in years. I got my deliverance and was into men from that point on. What I failed to know as a babe in Christ was that deliverance is not a one-time thing; if and when the enemy sees a door, he will open it and boy did this door swing wide open.

I didn't have romantic feelings for this woman is what I often tried to convince myself, but my heart called me a liar. She had become the first voice I wanted to hear in the morning and the last voice I wanted to hear at night. She would call or text me while serving her Pastor. I would lie to those around me about where I was going just to be with her all day. I gave up everything like the fool I was while dealing with this woman. I stopped preaching, I stopped mentoring, I stopped telling my testimony, I made no appearances; I was right where the devil wanted me to be. Till this day, I don't understand how Preachers can get in the pulpit and knowingly sin. I still held the title, but I sat myself down until I could figure out what the heck was going on with me. I turned down engagements and I barely spoke to my closest friends because I was so ashamed yet so caught up. I started drinking again after being a recovered alcoholic, hoping the liquor would silence my spirit while fueling my flesh. I was in such a dark place mentally, emotionally, spiritually and I thought she was the light. It was like I had been bewitched and totally lost myself in this woman. I was losing the little sense that I had left. How did I get here and what was it with her? What hoodoo did she put on me for me to get so lost in her lust? I was so infatuated with her yet disgusted with her at the same time. How could I kiss the same demon that I was trying to cast out?

The scary thing was this was not a sexual soul tie, and had it been I could have accepted that better and gotten free much faster, because sex for me was easy to get over, prostitution and porn taught me how to lose the emotional connection a long time ago. This was an emotional affair between two already emotional women with a familiar spirit. Because I had been with more women than men from an early age, she had become my comfort zone, being with her fit like a murderous glove.

I realized why the "relationship" was so intense.

Preaching In Pain

I was a known, I'll say lesbian, others may say bisexual, all of my serious relationships were with women, until I gave God a real yes. Being with men was an adjustment that I had to make according to my faith, and I was so on fire for God that I thought I was completely free. So many Preachers and people in church struggle with same-sex attraction and think getting married will cure it, it won't; and it doesn't mean the spirit is gone just because you haven't been sexually active. I was not aware then, that homosexuality and lesbianism is not a one night only recovery, it takes time to fully be delivered from that stronghold; but because I was so consumed with the things of God I forgot about the residue. When she came into my life, she was the residue that exposed what was still in me. When I realized that I was trying to suffocate my spirit with alcohol and her presence, I knew this had to end. My love for God had to supersede my lust for her. The enemy doesn't use new tricks, he always pulls out something old in a different season. He knew I would never go back to the strip club, he knew I wouldn't get strung out on drugs again, so he used something old, but unexpected to get me to fall, and it worked. However, my conviction could no longer be contained, and I knew this had to end.

I went to a church service one evening and the Prophet whispered in my ear and said, "The person you're connected to is a witch, sent on assignment to ruin your legacy. This person has conformed themselves into a light to deceive you, but in reality, they want to destroy your now and your next. God said, he allowed it for a season for a reason, but it is over now." I fell out on the floor and laid in a fetal position. I cried uncontrollably to the Lord, screaming at the top of my lungs, "Forgive me! Lord I want to be free!" I don't know how I allowed myself to get in this mess, but all I knew is I wanted out! I wanted my ministry back. I wanted my relationship with God back, but most importantly I wanted my sanity back because this took a toll on my mental health. She, however, was not on the same page and things got ugly.

We went back and forth during the time of our dealings, but when it was officially over, the sweet and shy lady I fell for turned into the demon she really was. Her true colors came out once it was evident that we could not be together. She became mean, disrespectful and hateful, she lied on me to her friends and she started dating another woman right away. It felt like the movie *Sleeping With The Enemy*, because that's what it was. I didn't really know who this person was. Now it was clear to me. This was no woman of God, she was planted in a church as an armor bearer and portrayed herself in a godly way just to make the connection, once the connection was made her job was complete. She no longer served as an armor bearer, she eventually left the church that I met her at and last I heard she was still dating women openly. I was reminded of the prophesy. A witch sent to steal my legacy. This had nothing to do with love, this was a blindsided attack. Sin will make you sleep with a snake. Whether knowingly or unknowingly she came with an agenda. The spirit that was operating in her was sent for one reason and one reason only, which was to destroy. Destroy my anointing, destroy my influence, destroy my legacy, so that I could be of no benefit to the Kingdom or those who God has and will assign to me. This was bigger than some lesbian entanglement this was sent to kill my assignment. That's why it was so hard to break, but I thank God for revealing the hidden motive and freeing me before it was too late.

I was young in age, young in ministry and I fell hard. Yeah, I was wrong, but I learned from all of my encounters. However, that needed to happen for me to know to not play with fire. She taught me that flesh could never be saved, it doesn't matter how long you've been in church or how much you love God your flesh can never and will never be saved or trusted. I thought that because I hadn't desired women in so long, I was safe to be around a lesbian. Please hear me loud and clear! If you play with fire you will get burned. The Bible says in, **2 Corinthians 6:17** Come out from among them and be separate, says the Lord. **1 Corinthians 15:33** Do not be deceived: "Evil company corrupts good habits. Even as leaders we must stay guarded, if that means being called mean or stuck up because you refuse to "hang" with people who are still involved with what you're trying to stay free from. Outside of the experience with her, being with the two Pastors revealed that my motive for marriage was not right and that I didn't need to use my body or dumb myself down for someone to pick me. All of these experiences were indeed painful and embarrassing, but they were necessary for my growth. I learned what not to do and refocused my attention back where it was supposed to be and that was on the Lord.

Chapter 6: Persecution

I decided that I still needed more healing and deliverance, which I continued to do away from the pulpit. Obviously, that meant no means of income at all from honorariums, book sales or seminars, so I got a job. I applied for the United States Post Office in Los Angeles and got hired. I hadn't had a real secular job since I was thirteen, so it was new, and I was trying to adjust since it did have a steady paycheck attached to it. I hadn't been in ministry long enough to have been recognized. Outside of a couple testimony videos going viral, I still wasn't easy to spot, or so I thought. I may not have been easy to spot from ministry, but unfortunately, I was recognizable from the porn movies. It may seem funny or even unbelievable, but truth is I no longer identified myself as a porn-star or a stripper. Once God removed me completely, I became a new creature in Christ. I don't even look the same, I don't think the same and my lifestyle was completely different. The issue with that was, I accepted my freedom from bondage, but others didn't, and they made sure to let me know.

While I was lost in the Shekinah Glory, I was quickly ejected by the unwanted opinions of those around me. I'm here working a job minding my own business and random people kept coming to my area staring and pointing, call me clueless, but I didn't catch on right away. I just thought that I was the new girl on the block and these guys were checking me out. Wrong! I was on an open platform for humiliation as they came to verify if I was the girl in the videos. My heart dropped to my knees as I said to myself with tears in my eyes, "Oh my God, they know." I stayed to myself a lot, not like I wanted to engage with people who were talking badly about me. I would eat in the cafeteria at a table by myself and they would sit across from me watching my videos on their cell phones, turning up the volume so I could hear it. I would smirk and put my earphones in as a way to calm myself down because these people just don't know that I will flip this table over and strangle the life out of them until they were able to tongue kiss the devil. I just put my earphones in and listened to Gospel music, to tune them out. Waking up for work became dreadful and everyday became a little more unbearable to walk in that facility. As the employees became more and more disrespectful, I decided that enough was enough. I went to HR, thinking they would solve the issue, but to my utter disgust and surprise, the chick in HR said it was my fault. My life choices and loud lipstick color brought the negative attention my way and her suggestion was that if no one physically touched me to just ignore it. "Are you serious?" was my question to her. She looked at me like yep I sure am. I got up and stormed out before I threw a chair at her head. I headed back to the work floor, walking past these ignorant people. Funny how everyone shared the porn videos, but no one shared the testimony videos. Why? Because it's better to laugh at someone else's sin and/or past transgression than to have to deal with your own. I felt like I was being bullied. I felt like a punk because I kept my mouth shut the whole time. Is this what Jesus meant when he said turn the other cheek? I would take long bathroom breaks and lock myself in the stalls, crying uncontrollably. Not so much because I was sad, but I was angry. Like big mad. I wanted to get them back! I was going to be the definition of going postal. I planned it out in my head too, I'm going to get a gun and shoot as many people as I can before postal police gets to me. They didn't know their lives were in danger as I plotted their murders every day, that's just how bad the torment became.

Since I wasn't active in ministry at the moment, I had much more time on my hands. That's when I found out that the internet can be a beast. My testimony had gone viral and I read the disturbing comments that people left about me. They wished death and disease on me, and let's not forget my favorite line, "Once a hoe, always a hoe" was constantly repeated. I guess in their minds I was wrong for telling the truth about the porn industry; how dare I speak negatively about what they find to be pleasurable. Speaking of the porn industry, my lovely former colleagues weren't so happy with me either. They behaved like the industry was some secret society and I broke the oath by outing the truth about what really goes on behind the scenes. It's a sick, demented and perverted business that uses you up and spits you out, leaving you physically and mentally impaired. They were mad and sent messages about what they would do if they "caught me in the streets". If they only knew that I was anticipating the reunion. All the pinned-up anger and frustration was waiting to be released and our little run in, in the streets would have been a memorable one, had it ever happened.

However, I still chose to turn the other cheek, not because I wanted to, but because I still had to represent God. Honestly, I think God was humbling me as well, because you can't be a leader and the only way you know how to confront is with cussing and cutting folks. I had to learn how to fight a different way, which was

Preaching In Pain

with my knees and not my fists, so I let them have this one. I knew this was a test that I had to past in order for God to get the Glory out of my life or even for me to ever be elevated. I failed the last test with ole girl, but this time I was watching the enemy's plots and plans to destroy my legacy. Yeah, it would have felt amazing to run them over in the parking lot, cuss them out and call their mama's a bunch of choice words, but it would've only been a temporary satisfaction with a forever consequence. So, the persecution continued, while I suffered in silence.

As I sat with my head down in the break room, I was tapped on my shoulder by my supervisor, Ronald McCord. He said, "The next time I see you, your head better not be down. Forget these miserable people! They have no lives and you have been the most entertainment they'll ever have. This job is their forever, but this is only a drop in the bucket for you because God is going to take you places you can only dream of. Don't let these miserable degenerates steal your joy." They may choose to ignore it, but I know you're a woman of God and your past is exactly that, your past. Cheer up and don't let me see you like this again." Then he walked away. First of all, who was he talking to? I must admit, I loved it. I hadn't received any comfort or encouraging words since I walked in that hell hole, so he was a breath of fresh air. I took into consideration everything he said and started walking in confidence again. Forget these people, I know who I am and who's I am! From that day forward, Mr. McCord changed my life, literally.

I was still riding solo at the job and Ronald would come check on me to make sure I was still smiling. We never flirted with each other, or did anything inappropriate, we just became really good friends. Although, immaturity would have people to believe that a man and woman cannot be strictly platonic, but at that time we were. After sitting down for some time, I finally started taking ministry engagements again and had one coming up in Barbados. Ronald was my friend and supervisor so I asked if he could give me the time off to do ministry and he said, "Only if you bring me something back." We laughed, and I agreed to bring him a souvenir from the Island. It felt good to be back on the road. Ministry was my lifeline and it fulfilled me to know that I was doing God's work and saving souls. Barbados was amazing and as promised, I got Ronald his souvenir. I waited for him to get to work and as soon as I saw him, I ran to him and said, "See I didn't forget about you, big head." As I handed him his gift. He smiled and asked me to take a walk with him and I did. He said, "I heard you had a book." "I do." I replied. "Well I want to buy it; I have daughters that need to hear your testimony." I gave him the price and went to my car to get the book. Before my shift was over, I went to his office and handed him the book, then clocked out for the night. I had two off days coming up, so I didn't see Mr. McCord until I returned back to his unit. Even though he and I were friends, he was still my supervisor, so when he called me into his office with a serious face, I was a little worried. As soon as I walked in, I said, "Whatever it is, I didn't do it!" There was a silence and then he said, "Close the door behind you." Oh shoot, I'm about to lose my little government job, I thought, but this conversation went to a place I wasn't prepared for.

"I read your book. Wow, you've been through a lot. You should let me take you on a date to show

you that every man is not as awful as you may think. From what I read and even from what I witnessed you go through in here, I know life has been hard for you, but you should give me a chance to be your Superman." I sat there in silence, thinking to myself, wow no one has ever said that to me, but he's probably just like the rest of them. Maybe not though, but what do I look like? Some damsel in distress waiting for a man to save me? I think not! He is kind of cute though and he is such a gentleman. I guess a date wouldn't hurt, plus I am kind of hungry.
"Ms. Williams?" He said. "Are you going to let me take you out or not?"
"Sure, when do you want to go?" I said.
"Now! Go clock out before the restaurant closes." Clock out! Now? I hated that place anyway, so he didn't have to tell me again. I ran to hit the clock and waited for him in the parking lot. We drove to one of my favorite spots by the Fox Hills Mall and talked for hours. I didn't have to hide my past because he already knew all about it. I didn't have to worry what he thought of me being an ex-everything because he was my friend first, he knew all about my past and still chose me. I had never been in love with a man before, had plenty

of them but never have I fallen in love, however, from that first night I felt something brewing for this man. I just didn't know how deep this love would flow.

They say that we are our worst enemies and I guess that is true because I just thought this was a temporary satisfaction as a favor to me for all the hell I had been through. I didn't think this was a permanent thing and I even expressed that to him. I told him I'd give this two years max. God had to check me about his son. How dare he give me a man of valor and I give him a time limit on our love. How dare I cry out for a man to love me and choose me to be his wife, but when God sends him, I reject it. Here this man is treating me like a queen, and choosing me knowing what I used to do, and who I used to be, but for some reason I couldn't fully accept his love. He did everything in his power to reassure me that my past was of no relevance to him. He didn't care, he saw the God in me and the woman I had blossomed into and he did his very best to show me that. He quickly tore down the walls I had built up from pain and distrust. I got lost in his love and accepted that he was the one for me and

Preaching In Pain

I was chosen for him. Too bad no one else saw it.

In the midst of that God-forsaken place, he was my breath of fresh air. People had already started rumors about us dating, but no one knew for sure and that's how we wanted to keep it. Nothing was made public until he proposed to me and the photo was posted on social media. Funny how none of them acknowledged me in person but seemed to stalk my Facebook page. The picture of him proposing was floating all over the post office rehashing more gossip from thousands of no life having miserable people. Ronald was swarmed by them all day and night telling him how crazy he was for wanting to be with me. Co-workers who he worked alongside him for many years stopped talking to him because he wanted me. Women all of a sudden started expressing their interest in him in hopes that he would leave me for them. I tried my best to not be petty, but they tried it. He was literally harassed daily and even demoted when they found out about our engagement. If dealing with the professional abuse wasn't enough, the moment he introduced me to his family all hell broke loose.

Preaching In Pain

I have dated men in the past who brought me around their children, their mothers and their friends and I have always been accepted and loved by them all. I didn't think things would be any different with Ron's family, but boy was I wrong. He is the youngest of four siblings and he had daughters from his first marriage. When he brought me around them, there was no warm welcome, there was no bond to be built for this great blended family that most would hope for. Instead, it was complete chaos and disrespect. He was very proud of who I had become, and he was excited about my ministry, so he didn't keep my testimony a secret. They knew all about me and used my past as a weapon to try to destroy not just our relationship, but my self-esteem. I was called a gold-digger and a whore because they could no longer use daddy as an ATM. I was accused of wanting to give him STD's and I may not be the sharpest knife in the drawer, but I do know that you can't give what you don't have. One of his siblings insisted that I was going to give him AIDS because of my past dealings in the sex industry. They constantly cursed me out, made fake social media pages to post my photos from my strip club days. When we finally married, we had an all-white wedding and one of his daughter's wore all black to my wedding. When I say all black, I mean a black dress, black shoes, black bag, black sunglasses and black lipstick. I remember one of his daughter's said if we'd ever have children together, my child would not be considered her sibling. My Bishop would even counsel me through this. He would tell me to turn the other cheek and let the Lord fight my battle; and when I tell you that I tried my very best and I do mean my very best to not let the Compton demon out of me, which I did very well until I just couldn't take it anymore. Here was another test and baby I failed miserably!

I was holding my peace at the job while being persecuted out of submission to God. I was holding my peace on the internet while being persecuted in the comment section. I was holding my peace with his family while being persecuted out of love for my husband, but you can only kick a dog so many times before it bites you back. I literally could not deal with the torment any longer. My final straw was the disrespect towards my husband. I am and have always been very loyal to those I love. Ronald and I are very opposite. I did a lot of dirt in the streets and lived a hard life, but he didn't. He was the "good guy". He got married young and had a family, started a career and tried to be an example of a good black man, not just to his children, but to his peers. We are not cut from the same cloth, but hey they say opposites attract. With that being said, I felt like he was being bullied because he chose to love me in spite of, and it pissed me off! See, it's one thing to hurt and mistreat me, but it's another thing to hurt what I love. The day that I saw the tears fall down his face because he was so hurt, shocked and disgusted by the way his colleagues, his friends and his family behaved, was the day I lost my religion. Minister who? Nothing about me was godly after that. Yes, I came out of the anointing and turned into a demon. I lost it! One of his daughter's called me a hoe for seven-hundredth time and I snapped. I said every foul thing I could and had this taken place in person and not on the phone, we'd both still be in jail. One of his sister's said it would be over her dead body if her brother stayed married to me and I kindly suggested that we go casket shopping. A female employee got mad and called Ron some nasty names while insulting me at the same time, so I jumped on a forklift and proceeded to run her over, (don't worry she's alright.) I had lost my mind. Everything that I bottled up, everything I tried to suppress and for every tear I cried as a result of the humiliation and persecution had come out swinging full force. "She's saying and doing all of that and she's supposed to be a Preacher." Funny how they wanted to acknowledge that I was a Minister now that I've come down to their level, but when I turned the other cheek and prayed for my enemies I was a dirty hoe. I didn't care anymore; I justified this rampage. I deserved to knock a few ninjas out for how they treated me while I was minding my business. If you ever saw the movie *Carrie*, it's about a teenage girl who was bullied and taunted, but she had demonic powers and when they went to prom they bullied her for the last time and she killed every last one of them. I watched that movie numerous times and didn't feel bad for not one person, that's what they get for messing with people and in this season I'm Carrie so what's up!

I just became so angry and that old man that I call the Compton demon rose. That ghetto, ignorant, violent, always ready to fight demon had risen from the dead. Even in my anger, I still heard the Lord's voice saying hold my peace and he will fight my battles, but the more he said it the angrier I got. The Lord was taking too long, and I needed these folks to get got right now! I felt like Peter and I was ready to cut an ear off. Lord, I'm sorry, but you're letting these people get a little too out of hand. I tried to be quiet, I tried to be godly, I tried to turn the other cheek, I tried to pray, now I'm ready to bust windows, tires and heads. Outside of the disrespect to my husband, what angered me the most was these people professed to know God. Some were Deacons in their church! How can you leave the house of God and come to work to harass me? Some of these people were active in their church and were seasoned Christians, but you are holding me hostage to my past transgressions? You're insulting my husband for being able to see beyond who I used to be and choosing to love who God created me to be? You can praise God for David, Paul and the Woman at the Well, but not receive me? So, Jesus can heal the sick, cast out demons, do many signs and wonders, but he can't save a chick that was in the porn industry? I was appalled and ready to fight. I knew they were waiting for any slip up, but I didn't care anymore. When I tried to show the love of God, I was still persecuted and rejected, so now it is what it is. The gloves are off!

The war between work and my in-laws had took a toll on my new marriage. Although, I was Ron's wife, they are still his family and he was put in a hard situation. He tried to keep peace, but there was none. He tried to bring us together, but he knew the tension was so high, tables would've start flying. I must admit, because I couldn't get to them, I took a lot of my frustration out on him and a wedge was created. I offered to annul the marriage because had I stayed in it, he would have left me anyway because I was planning on retaliating violently towards his people, yeah it got that bad. Their goal was to cause us to divorce and they almost won. Because I was not in my right mind to make logical decisions, my husband prayed earnestly to keep this marriage together. I felt that leaving him was the only answer to stop the persecution for both of us, even though my heart didn't want to let him go, but for my sanity and his I needed to walk away. My fairytale love story had turned dark and vicious. Never in a million years did I think this would be my life. Out of all the dealings I had with someone's family, this by far was the worst one. They were trying to steal my happiness because they didn't think an ex-pornstar deserved a perfect ending. Here they are miserable, with multiple baby father's, several ex-wives, no one to come home to, can't keep a man even if they paid one, and I get the good guy. They did everything in their power to try to snatch my blessing away.

I remember going to sleep and God showed me Atlanta, GA. I ignored it because I didn't understand what he wanted me to get from that, but from that night on Atlanta popped up everywhere. I would look at a newspaper, it was an article about Atlanta. I would turn on the television and it was an Atlanta based show on. I really couldn't shake this city out of my spirit.

Was God calling us to Atlanta as a way of escape? I brought it to my husband's attention, and he was in agreement for us to move. We knew we had to leave, in order to save our marriage and my ministry there had to be distance between us and them for a while. Not to mention, Atlanta was considered the "Black Hollywood". I had my first book, I wrote a play, a reality show and even a movie, so this may be a good idea. Three months later, we packed our bags, left Los Angeles and moved to Atlanta.

Chapter 7 - Judas

Outside of my home church in Los Angeles, I never had many ministry friends or spiritual brothers and sisters until I came to Atlanta and started doing ministry full time again. As I began to host conferences and revivals, I started meeting many people in the ministry and this was new for me. When I was on the road, I was in and out, so there were no real friendships, sisterhoods or brotherhoods established. The more I hosted events, the more I met different people and call me naïve, but I really believed these people were saved for real. I mean they were armor bearers, first ladies, Ministers and seasoned people in the Gospel. I was in a new location and building my brand, so I was open to the new relationships. I was actually looking forward to it as my husband and I were basically starting from scratch. However, after engaging with these folks I should've stayed to myself from the beginning.

Although, I had been in ministry for some time, this was the first time I started hosting my own conferences, revivals and events. I was in need of an armor bearer, but didn't know where to start. I never did this before, do I send out a tweet or an application, like how do you find an armor bearer. I just prayed about it and asked the Lord to lead me. I had a preaching engagement in another state and "Tatum" was assigned as my armor bearer during my stay. This young lady and I hit it off immediately. I was drawn to what turned out to be a lie, but it was the image of innocence, purity and her zeal for God that captivated me. We remained in contact through social media. I heard the Lord call her name and assumed she was the one that he chose as my armor bearer, when in reality he was probably

Preaching In Pain

warning me to stay away. I talked to her about it and she was excited and in agreement. My preaching itinerary began to increase, which meant she would need to be close; I had a big empty home in Atlanta and invited her to move in. A major conference of mine was coming up and this would be her first assignment. The moment she arrived, I knew immediately that I should've ran the other direction the moment she showed up with a bonafide witch. Unbeknownst to me she belonged to a weirdo at that time. The woman she called her spiritual mother was very demonic, controlling, psychotic, and this lady was into some dark stuff and had no plans on releasing her to do anything in my ministry. While at the conference she prohibited Tatum from being active, she literally didn't let her move or even speak to me. Most would have had sympathy for this situation, but I didn't. I starred at the puppet and puppet master from the stage trying not to throw a shoe at both of them. Um ma'am, what is this and why did you even come, were the burning questions in my head. Tatum knew she had a soul tie with a wicked woman and coming under my leadership would cause drama which I have no time for, but when people are chasing a platform and not an assignment by God, they don't care who they put in harm's way. Now I have all this unnecessary warfare and had to fight a witch in the spirit behind someone else's ulterior motive. She should've declined any offers from me, but it appeared to her as though my platform could get her to places that her mama-witch couldn't. During the entire conference this lady had Tatum by a short leash and in my mind, this short relationship between my armor bearer and I had ended before it ever really began, and I was absolutely ok with that.

The conference had ended, and it was back to business as usual. Not long after I received countless texts and inboxes from Tatum, apologizing for what took place, her mother even called to apologize and give me the scoop on the witch. She cried, she begged, she promised, and my forgiving heart listened and believed her. She wanted me to reconsider her as my armor bearer as she insisted that she cut off all contact with the mama-witch. I should've hung up and deleted all contact; as the great poet *Maya Angelou* quoted, "When someone shows you who they are, believe them the first time." I had a glimpse of her true nature, but was still blinded by the performance, the sweet and innocent girl role. So, I made excuses for her, "she is being controlled," "she doesn't know any better," "she may be fearful of the witch," and blah, blah, blah. I tried not to believe what my eyes were showing me because I wanted to only see the good in her, so I gave her another chance. Those who witnessed the debacle at the conference strongly urged me not to have anything to do with her, but I ignored their counsel and I welcomed her in with a clean slate. She would fly in from her city to meet me wherever I was speaking at, as we were trying to reestablish our bond. She told me her living situation, she was unhappy with how she was being treated and she was sleeping on the floor. Knowing I was going to be "Captain Save-Em", I got the hint and offered to move her to Atlanta once again. She was now a spiritual daughter and I couldn't have her in a situation like that. My door was open, and she didn't need anything, but the clothes on her back and that's exactly what she came with, clothes and a broken TV. She didn't have to worry about sleeping on a living room floor because she had her own room and her own bathroom that I decorated in her favorite color. Although, she was in her early twenties, I treated her like my child. I cooked for her, I provided for her, and I loved her, but that love was not returned because it was never established.

As we began to do more assignments together, I noticed she wasn't as sharp as she had been in the beginning. She would forget my glasses, leave my stuff at the church I ministered at, and just drop the ball in her servitude. I operate in a spirit of excellence and I am no non-sense when it comes to ministry, so I'm not fond of many errors. I quickly found out that she couldn't focus on serving because she wanted to do the leading. All of a sudden, she had books to release and was taking ministry engagements. First of all, I just got you from a whole witch, literally, this lady was into witchcraft. Tatum's spirit needed to be prayed back into a pure place with God because it was tainted by this woman she just left; and she had no ministerial training whatsoever to be taking on engagements. What is this? She needed deliverance, not a mic. I was not in agreement with that and I explained to her anything you birth prematurely is subject to die, let God deliver you from all the filth you just came out of, let him renew your mind and spirit, then you can go and minister to others who have gone through the same things. When God anointed David, he was not king the next week. I assured her that I would help cultivate her gift and when the time was right, she would be released to minister, but what you cannot do is have your open wounds bleed out on the people and think I'm going to condone that. Needless to say, she was not happy with my suggestion or my correction. She instantly became rebellious and standoff-ish as her plans didn't seem to work over here and the close nit bond wasn't so close anymore.

Not long after, I booked a singer for my conference and we became cordial, she invited me to her parent's church. Her mother was a Prophetess in the church and her father was an Apostle. I decided to slide through because I wanted to hear this girl sing again. She was the praise and worship leader of the house and she had the voice of an Angel, outside of her singing I actually enjoyed the service that day. Not long

Preaching In Pain

after, I brought Tatum and my husband to the church a few times and they enjoyed it as well. The Prophetess and Apostle had many daughters, and some were around Tatum's age; they began a friendship and sisterhood which I encouraged because she didn't have anyone in Atlanta other than me and I wasn't her friend, I was her covering. I had no issue with the girls hanging out, but I noticed that Tatum was spending a lot of time with the Prophetess and serving her ministry needs. Meanwhile, she's failing to serve my ministry while living in my house. Tatum took to the Prophetess and Apostle because they quickly gave her a mic which is what she was thirsty for. She didn't want to serve, she wanted to be in the front and the moment they gave her an opportunity she ran with it. I was taken back that a seasoned woman in the church would allow another Minister's armor bearer to serve her ministry while failing and rebelling against her own leader. Then again, I do know why, their church was very small and didn't have many members outside of their children and grandchildren, so they would do anything, even if that meant being out of order to have a seat filler and an extra hand.

Preaching In Pain

The final straw was during another one of my conferences in Atlanta. Tatum purposely did things to hinder the flow of the service, she had an attitude that was big enough to be noticed by other people. She left the service to go out to eat with the Prophetess and Apostle while I was left to not only preach and host an entire event, but now I had to do what was supposed to be her job as well. It took everything in me not to fire off on this little girl. Here I was taking care of her, feeding her, providing for her, trying to instill values in her as a woman, moved her in my home and now you turn on me at another one of my conferences'! I should have known better the first time when she came with the witch, whom she said she cut off only to find out that was a lie. She stayed in contact with this woman and I wondered was this a plot. Were they in cahoots? Did the mama-witch tell her to get all she could from me as a benefit for the both of them? Seems like it, since I found out that Tatum had secretly saved a lot of my ministry contacts in order to get herself booked. I couldn't believe it. This little sweet and innocent persona was all a fraud. They say you have to watch the quiet ones because they end up being the worse ones, and in this case, that was the truth.

Enough was enough and if I didn't release her and get her away from me, I may have lost my Holy Ghost. I prayed and asked God to humble me before I had this discussion because even though I had every right to be upset by the betrayal and blatant disrespect, I'm still a leader and had to handle this as such. I asked her if we could talk, she said yes. I told her that her behavior was foul, hurtful, and unacceptable. With tears in my eyes, I expressed the hurt, after everything that I had done for her, allowing her back in even after the first situation and to be repaid with this was heartbreaking. She sat there in silence and I released her from my ministry, since she wanted to be the forefront of an empty church so bad, she got what she wanted. Being that I moved her from another state, I still felt responsible for her, so I offered to help her find an apartment and I would pay half the rent for a few months until she got on her feet. She agreed and I thought we were on the same page. Wrong!

A few days later, I came home, and her things were packed with a note left on the table. She thanked us for everything and placed the house key I gave her next to the note. I was confused as to where she went so fast, but then again, I was relieved that this was over. I later got a phone call from Tatum's mother and the Prophetess she was so fond of. This young lady left with a lie on her tongue and a plan in her hand. She called her people and told them I put her out of my house, and she was homeless with nowhere to go in these Atlanta streets by herself. I was floored. The Prophetess quickly provided shelter for her new spiritual daughter, which is what she ultimately wanted. So, not only did you try to use me as a come up, play me, disregard my ministry for someone else's while in my house, you lie on me too. Oh ok, so if this is what having an armor bearer feels like, I don't ever need another one.

Speaking of the Prophetess, I saw why Tatum

was so fond of her. She traded in one witch for another one. I didn't know how wicked this woman could be and how she had more of a cult than an actual church because her children, grandchildren and the other six members worshiped her; her way was right, and she did no wrong in their eyes. Prophetess Jezebel should be her name because she operated in a spirit of control and manipulation and anyone with spiritual sense could see it. Her ways were slowly seeping out, but I knew she was foul by the way she gladly stole my armor bearer, truth be told she probably encouraged Tatum's rebelliousness. However, before the drama took its full course, I was in relationship with two of her seventeen daughters. Her daughter "Erin" had a lot of children and was currently pregnant with another. It was no secret that I had issues with fertility. I have spoken about my struggle publicly on many occasions. Erin knew of my desire to have children and she needed an extra hand as she was preparing to have another mouth to feed. I was elated the moment she asked me to be the Godmother to her unborn

Preaching In Pain

child. Lord knows motherhood was something I longed for and if I couldn't love my own, I'd love someone else's.

I got the call that she was in labor and I ran to the hospital. Was there for hours before it was time for her to push my little Angel out. I grabbed one leg and her husband grabbed the other as she birthed this beautiful baby girl. I fell in love with her instantly. She had my love even before she was born, but the moment I held her my heart stopped aching. As soon as she was just three weeks old, I started picking her up and keeping her for days at a time. I provided her clothes, medicine and whatever else she needed because Erin was already struggling with the other children, but I made it clear she didn't have to worry about this one. This was my baby girl, and she wouldn't have to worry about anything. Outside of taking care of the baby, Erin would ask me for money for the other children as well as household needs and without question, I gave it to her. When Tatum moved out, I was getting ready to turn her room into a nursery for my

Preaching In Pain

Goddaughter, but unfortunately that did not happen.

With the fallen out that took place with the Prophetess and Tatum, my husband and I decided to no longer visit their church for obvious reasons but leaving the church didn't mean leaving the baby. I had a conversation with Erin about us not returning, but I would still be very present in my Goddaughter's life. She allowed me to still see the baby and she continued to receive money from me. I guess the Prophetess wasn't satisfied with just taking my armor bearer, she wanted to hit me where it really hurt. Erin lived with her parents and suddenly, she wasn't calling for me to get the baby as much, she was giving me excuses as to why I couldn't pick her up. I called her with some stern words and basically told her don't play me with this kid, just because I don't want to attend your mother's church anymore doesn't mean you use the child as a weapon. She insisted that she wouldn't do me like that, but at the end of the

Preaching In Pain

day, she did me like that.

Weeks went by and I wasn't able to see the baby. I got the hint and packed all her clothes, formula, blankets, etc., that was at my home and drove to their house. It took everything in me not to drive my car through the front door because I was livid. Not only did this lady play a role in the destruction between Tatum and I, but she told her daughter to not let me see the baby and I was ready to hurt these people. Anger consumed me, but not more than the pain and heartache. They knew I couldn't have children. They knew I loved this baby and had financially taken care of her from the moment she was born. They did this out of spite. When I got back home and walked into the empty room that I was preparing for the baby, I dropped to the floor and cried like someone had died. I hadn't felt that kind of pain in a long time and I screamed until I had no voice. I already dealt with the depression of not being able to bear a child of my own, and here it is a baby was given to me and then snatched from me by church folks; these were preachers for crying out loud! She had lots of kids, so she didn't know the pain of a barren woman. This so-called woman of God had taken my armor bearer who I considered as a spiritual daughter and then she took my Goddaughter and only God himself stopped me from doing what I really wanted to do. However, I wiped my tears and put those people behind me and just kept preaching through the pain.

After that whole ordeal I was over people and didn't even entertain the thought of an armor bearer. Ministry engagements were still coming in often and I must admit it's hard being on the road with no help, but I was maintaining to the best of my abilities. At the same conference that Tatum acted a fool at, I met a woman by the name of "Lisa" who came from another country to fellowship with us. By this time, I had accumulated a lot of social media followers and she happened to be one of them. She caught my attention when she shared that she had recently lost her job, but still trusted God to make away. She didn't allow unemployment to stop her from getting what God had for her, so she said. Nonetheless, I was impressed by her faith, not many people will travel down the street after losing a job, let alone to another country. I don't meet with everyone I come in contact with, but I felt the need to meet with Lisa after the conference before she left and let her know that I was honored that she came and fellowshipped with us given the circumstance. She seemed to be a little nervous by my presence, but I cracked jokes as I always do to loosen her up. As she got comfortable, she made it a point to tell me how much money she sowed into the conference and I thanked her for her support. She asked if we could stay in contact and I had no problem with that. We spoke often through social media and she wanted me to inform her of all my upcoming events, which I did. I believe it was just three months after the conference that I held a revival, and she came to that as well, once again traveling from overseas. This time she stayed a few days after and invited me to lunch. Once I arrived, she expressed that she wanted me to be her covering and spiritual mother. After just dealing with Tatum's shenanigans in my head, I screamed, "HECK NO!" But I'm always reminded to not make someone pay for the mistakes of someone else. I should have still declined, but she came off as a really nice woman who just wanted a little more Jesus. I convinced myself that this wouldn't be a repeat of Tatum and I was right; it wasn't a repeat, it was far worse.

Lisa and I began talking frequently and she would come to Atlanta often. She was a big help to my ministry financially as she always sowed seeds and offered to help with ministerial needs. We went to a church and the Prophetess stated that when Lisa moved stateside, the Lord will have her to be my armor bearer and I will help her in many ways both naturally and spiritually. However, prophecy is conditional, and those who do not activate works with their faith or the word may not see it come to past. Lisa was limited by an unbelieving husband who wasn't so fond of me or her new Christian lifestyle. As she travelled and spent time with me on ministry assignments, her behavior changed and she wanted to fast and pray more and live by Biblical principles; but her spiritual growth made him angry, at least that's what was told to me. I was understanding to the fact that these new changes would take some getting used to and would pray for him and their marriage. Lisa informed me that her husband participated in seances and consulted with mediums. I knew then that this would be a major problem. How could we advance in ministry together if you have a warlock for a husband? I was feeling sorry for her, thinking he was hindering her journey with God, but that was not the real reason for his discomfort.

At that time, I was travelling often and was preparing to do my first production. I was turning my story *From Porn To The Pulpit* into a stage play. Most people would think that theatre and film will bring in big bucks, and in most cases that is true, once you get established and sell out multiple arenas. However, I was just getting started and although we sold out the first two shows, we had to invest that money into the next city because we had no sponsors or investors, not even a seed sower. Lisa told her husband that she was about to blow up and make big bucks by being involved with not just my ministry but my production as well. No wonder why he didn't like me, she wasn't making the money she lied to him about. He's seeing all this traveling, but she's not bringing any money back like she claimed she would. Meanwhile, I'm in the dark. This was no spiritual journey for her, I was just a come up, an opportunity for her to make money since she lost her job. Whole time I'm thinking she was genuinely serving, sowing and supporting, but this was just another scheme. A get rich quick plan and she was using me to do it!

One of my worse qualities is giving people the benefit of the doubt and trying to believe what my eyes are not seeing. I didn't want to believe she was a conniving, manipulative, wolf in sheep clothing. This couldn't be happening again! I let someone else in despite my reservations and they played me again. Tatum wanted a platform, Lisa wanted money and I fell for the same plot. The innocence, the hunger for God, the want to help me do ministry was all a lie. Where the heck was my discernment? Lisa was a great actress until she couldn't play the role anymore. The money from the production didn't come in as expected and her true colors came out. When we first met, she made it a point to tell me how much money she sowed to the conferences and would always sow seeds and offer to take on the financial responsibilities of the ministry as she, and I quote, was led by God. She claimed it was because I was her spiritual mother and God told her to sow on good ground. I remember sharing a story with her about how I was leery in receiving large donations from people because some folks will use that as a way to get what they want. I remember a lady gave a large donation to my ministry and thought she paid her way for some gay sex. Um, no to you! Needless to say, I'm grateful for donations and seeds, but I be side eyeing too.

Preaching In Pain

Lisa swore up and down she wasn't like that, it was God who told her to sow, but last time I checked God wouldn't tell you to pluck up seed that he told you to put in the ground. This lady was so angry that she couldn't profit off of the Prophet and had now said that all of her donations to the ministry were not donations or seed offerings, but they were loans. Now, I have encountered many demons, but never in my entire saved life have I seen one like this. Are you kidding me! I've labored with this woman, prayed for this woman, fasted for this woman because of the secret battles that she had, invited her into my personal space, taught her how to operate in ministry properly, had her back in the natural and in the spirit and for what? For it all to be a bald-headed lie and plot to make money off of me! Here I am standing in the gap and warring for someone who was never on my side. She used her money as a way to manipulate ministries. I found out she would seed large amounts to get in good and when things didn't go her way, she cried church hurt. How in the world could I see for everybody else except my own self? I had Judas in the camp multiple times and was blinded by their representative, I was blinded by who they wanted me to see and when I finally find out who they really were it was too late.

There are not many people that I despised and I'm not proud to say that Lisa had become that one. I needed God to check my spirit quick because not only was I angry, but I was full of retaliation. I'd turned the other cheek so many times, but this time I wanted to hurt her bad. I didn't care nothing about her being the same height as an NBA player, I can climb trees and wear out giants. My anger was more so kindled towards her because I explained my hurt to her, I told her what I went through with Tatum and just with people in general within ministry and she swore she wasn't like that. They say nothing hurts more than getting hurt by the one you explained your hurt to. I was opening myself up to a snake from day one. I was loving on the very people who were plotting against me and I was disappointed in myself because I couldn't see it.

These chicks have given armor bearer's a bad name in my book and I was no longer entertaining the idea of having one, but when God removes, he also replaces. Who I needed wasn't far off, and that was Melissa. She started off as just a supporter, showing up to my events, buying my books and was always present. Every time I looked up, she was there. She would offer her services and lend a hand with no ulterior motive, she wasn't looking to get paid or be seen; she just wanted to serve; but I was so wrapped up with Judas that I didn't recognize a real one. She was hidden in plain sight and although I tore down the idea of ever having another armor bearer, she still fulfilled the role and is still with me today. I never had to question her love or loyalty all these years, she's been solid and I'm grateful that she showed me what real servitude looks like, despite my walls being up. I wasn't always the easiest to deal with especially after being played multiple times by women in ministry. God will give you who you need and what you need even when you don't want it.

With all that happens within ministry, you need an outlet, like a buddy you can let your hair down with; and that's what I had in "Ericka". I met her doing ministry as well, but she was no armor bearer. She was a certified boss who put on women empowering events in the Atlanta area and we instantly connected. For those who know me personally, know that I am a jokester and love to laugh, so was Ericka. She was business oriented, but super funny and we became close fast. She was married with a son and her husband and my husband would hang out often. Outside of our silly personalities and love for God, we shared the same issue which was infertility. Ericka had many miscarriages before and even after her son, she longed for more children, but was unable to have a full-term pregnancy. I was completely barren with no children at the time and oddly enough that was our common bond. I was so happy we met because I was praying for a saved married couple for my husband and I to connect with, for double dates and game nights, so this was a blessing or at least is started off that way.

I should've known something was wrong when she fell out with every friend she had introduced me to. She started out with ten sister-friends when we first met and then she was down to three in just a few months. Sometimes God will remove multiple people out of your life, but if you fall out with everyone you come in contact with, sis it may just be you. Funny thing is she admitted the fallouts were her fault and I should've braced myself for this Bipolar Baptist the moment we went to lunch and she said none of her friendships lasted more than two years, as we were not far from the two year mark. However, I thought for some reason it would be different with us being that we were so close. She had become my Atlanta bestie and we were inseparable. I adored her son, and we shared many laughs, but the same one that'll make you laugh, will turn around and make you cry.

Preaching In Pain

Lord knows I've been a lot of things, but jealous or in secret competition with someone has never been a part of my DNA. There's room at the top for us all and I want everyone to win, but that's not the case for everyone. It seemed like Ericka was there for me the most when I took loses or was going through personal battles, but when things were going well for me, she wasn't as present. I noticed some things, but after going through failed friendships since I got to Georgia, I was desperately hoping that this would work, so I overlooked a lot of red flags. Her behavior was weird, she was snappy and "sometimey", but I would just make excuses for her and said she's been through a lot, that's why she is the way she is. But that's exactly what they were, excuses.

Again, when I was down and out, Ericka was my shoulder to cry on, but the moment things were going great, that shoulder was no longer available. I got to the point where I was no longer making an effort to prove I was a real friend. I felt like we were turning into a couple (without the sex) and I was always trying to prove my love and loyalty so she could feel safe, but it was not returned. I still considered her a friend, but I wasn't going to force anything. My annual conference was approaching, and Ericka had a building that she rented out. That particular year, I didn't have the large budget that I previously had to rent a venue space that cost thousands of dollars, so she offered to rent me her building. I was grateful and advertised that the conference would be held at her location. Maybe two weeks before the conference, my Bipolar bestie decided to make life difficult for me. Mind you I have rented her building out multiple times for different events and there has never been an issue, but this time I met the real Ericka. She had her assistant contact me and ask me to give a large deposit, get insurance and a host of other non-sense. Here I am lost in the sauce. We never communicate through a third party and why bring this on me last minute. It didn't just stop there, she took this social media. Ericka has what we call "Twitter fingers", she loves to post subliminal messages online and I've known her to do it to others including to her spouse, but once again my silly self, thought we were closer than that. She was my sis, my ace, my Atlanta bestie, surely she wouldn't treat me like the other people I've seen her dog out, not this woman of God, not this boss, but Ericka taught me that it didn't matter what your social status was or how much money you claim to have, demons don't discriminate and all they need is a body, anybody.

There was obvious tension between her and I during this time, because I didn't understand why she was doing me like that. I had to still be high from all the drugs I used to take back in the day because I still tried to make excuses for her and find some reasoning for this uncanny behavior. To be honest, just because I was angry with her didn't automatically erase all that we have built, the love was still there it was just being suffocating by her demons. Even though she showed her natural black tail, I figured we were going to get through the conference, wait a few days and either she would call me to apologize or I would call her to cuss her out, but nevertheless I never thought things would have gotten as bad as they did.

The woman of God in me always supersedes the thug in me, so I approached this from a humble and saved place. I texted Ericka the morning of the conference and said, "I don't know what's going on with us, but none of it matters at this point. We have a bigger assignment to complete and that's a Kingdom assignment, so whatever I have done to you, I apologize. Let's not let anything interfere with the move of God this weekend." There was no response. I was ok with that; I gave it to God and got ready for the conference. People from all over the world came here, some flew in, some drove near and far, the place was packed. We had our first service on a Friday night, and it was amazing, despite the intentional distractions from Ericka. She continued to walk in and out of the service, she purposely did not provide toilet paper or towels for my guest, and before the Preacher got off stage good, she sent her puppet to collect the money. The funds were not counted yet and I explained that to Ericka's assistant. I told her that I would send the money once we finished the count, she agreed, and we left to prepare for the next service which was at 2pm the next day. Ericka was paid in full that night, so you could only imagine my astonishment when Melissa called to tell me that the doors were locked and there was an event happening in the building that I paid my "friend" in full and booked months ago. "I'm sorry what?" "The doors are locked, and Ericka said the conference is cancelled because you took too long to pay last night and there is a party going on right now." This could not be true; she did not take my money and then lock the doors. She did not cancel my conference while hundreds of people have paid registration, bought flights, rental cars and hotels to be here. No this can't be happening. My husband called Ericka and asked was it true, was she really doing this and if so why. She flat out told him that she didn't give a "F" about me or my conference, she'll send the money back because it's shut down. Ron was flabbergasted this was our friend, our sister! He then said, but what about all the people that came out here for this, she responded again with she didn't give a "F" about those people either, it was cancelled and that was that. Ron even called her husband, you know our friend and brother in Christ, but he purposely didn't answer. I called Ericka myself and of course there was no answer, so I called her assistant because she played a dirty hand in this too and once I got confirmation that they were not letting us continue the conference, I was on my way to jail to start that prison ministry I always joke about! I jumped in my car and ran stop lights trying to get to her. Since she locked the doors, my plan was to drive my car into them, find her and hurt her bad. I mean what else did I have to lose? She just ruined my conference, my name and my brand and had the audacity to say she didn't give a "F" about me or the people of God. I was livid, these people trusted me enough to spend their money, take off of work and travel to a place they've never been because they trusted the God in me. Some of these people were fed up, barely holding on and even suicidal, but they were giving God and life one more shot by coming to my conference and she locked them out for no reason! I wanted blood, literally! In all my life, I have never been that irate, I was at a point where I didn't care about jail or any consequences for what was about to take place that day. As a Minister of the Gospel, I hate to admit that I wanted to drag this chick and I found justification in my reasonings. This was not done by an enemy or even a stranger, this was done by someone I called friend. This was done by someone I loved and laughed with. This was done by someone that I prayed for and worshiped with. She tried to ruin my name and my brand and for the life of me I did not know why. I would have found some kind of understanding in all of this, if we had a falling out or a major argument prior, but nothing. We had no falling out, we had no beef prior to this conference. There was no just cause for this! If Judas needed a face it would be hers.

As I sped down the street to commit a crime of passion, I was stopped by the sound of my spiritual mother's voice as she screamed through the phone, "Danielle, don't do it! She's trying to kill your baby!" Oh yeah, I was eight months pregnant with the baby they said I would never have when all of this took place. The same woman who planned my gender reveal just a few months prior, the same woman that was supposed to be the Godmother to my son, was the same woman who wanted me to lose my baby and my brand; and I realized why. When we met, one of our connections was because we were both barren, but low and behold God breathes life into my dead wound and all of a sudden, she distances herself. Friday night her building was packed with people that came for my event, which she hadn't been able to get a full house for her own events. On top of that I was on her stage pregnant and glowing which was something she was also struggling to do. Not to mention, she wanted a relationship with my spiritual mother, but mother couldn't stand Ericka. Could it be that my successes enraged her to this point? When I found out I was pregnant, we were all excited and worried at the same time because I could never carry a child full term, six months was the longest I could go. She was very supportive as I received negative reports from the doctors about my unborn child, she was very supportive when it looked like things were going wrong with the pregnancy, so she threw me a beautiful gender reveal party as a special memory to have because she didn't really think I'd be able to have this baby. However, God made sure I recovered from every loss in ministry by selling out the conference and by allowing me to endure my pregnancy full term. She had a front row seat to all of this, and it brought out the ugliest demon in her. She had more money than me, a bigger house than I did, and a multi-million-dollar business she was running, but she still was not genuinely happy or fulfilled because she did not have the true desires of her heart. **Song of Solomon 8:6,** states that jealousy is cruel as the grave. Meanwhile, I forgot I was pregnant as I was still driving to kill her and burn down the building she locked me out of. Shoot if we couldn't have our service in there nobody could because it was getting burned down that day.

Preaching In Pain

What I didn't mention in the previous statements of her dropping "F" bombs, she not only said F my conference which made me angry, she not only said F the people of God that came to the conference which made me livid, but when Ron asked why are you doing this, you know she's eight months pregnant, little Ms. Ma'am said she didn't give an F about my baby! I can't tell you what transpired from the words coming out of her mouth to me getting in the car heading her way. I just saw red. My stomach tensed up so bad and it was hard as a rock, but I was so angry I forgot he was in there. I can't even tell you how my spiritual mother got on my phone, but the moment I heard her scream, "Your baby, think about your baby!" I stopped abruptly. Had I not been pregnant, I would most definitely be writing this book from a prison cell. I thank God for my son, and she should thank God for him too, because the same baby she cursed, actually saved her life, literally!

Even in all of my hatred and animosity, I still covered Ericka. I don't believe in going live on social media and exposing people. Instead, I went live and lied to cover her. I told everyone that we had exceeded capacity for the building we were in the following night and we would be fellowshipping at another location with a bigger space. That was a lie, but it was better than the truth. I had to take the hit as the vendors were upset with me because she locked their products in the building and told them to pick them up Monday. I had to take the hit from out of town guests who didn't know where the new location was because Ericka took the sign off the door. I had to take the hit financially and spend every dime that was raised the night before, plus our own savings to pay for another location that charged me a ridiculous amount of money and only had a few hours to do it; all while being eight months pregnant. I still never said a word publicly about what really took place.

None of my ministry relationships seemed to flourish as I have met many women who hold titles. Seems like we would connect and for whatever reason the communication would fade or there'd be a disagreement, some type of hidden jealousy or competition, even some lesbian attractions that I was no longer interested in or falling for, but nothing cut me deeper than this. Yes, I was irate, but I was devastated more than anything else. I would have been content if this was done by anybody else, but not her because I loved this lady from such a genuine place. I thought she was my friend, and this hurt me so bad because I still to this day never got a real answer. How could someone so close to me do me like this? I've met plenty of scandalous people in my life, but no "friend" has ever broken my heart like this. I remember that following Monday night, I was at my mother's house getting ready to go to another event. As I was showering everything just hit me at once. In my mind, my brand was destroyed, who would want to come and support another one of my events? Because of all the money we had to spend on the other location on top of the money that was already paid to her, I was unable to get the things I needed for my son at that moment. I was embarrassed, I was hurt, I was confused, and completely broke down. I almost collapsed in the shower as I burst out in tears, my mother grabbed me and helped me out, as she was feeling sorry for me, her anger towards Ericka was reaching uncontainable levels. We're from Compton and I'm her daughter, so her reaction was fitting, however I had to stop my mom from catching a case.

Tatum, Erin, Prophetess Jezebel, Lisa and Ericka were my introduction to what betrayal actually looked like. I had every right to be upset, hurt and even angry, but once those emotions subsided, I had to thank God for my encounters with these people because they all taught me lessons about myself. One thing I learned from them all was to not expect everybody to have the same heart and motive as you. Also, stop being so quick to pull strangers in so closely without discernment or assurance from the Holy Spirit, for the Bible says in **Matthew 7:16**, you will know them by their fruits. You have to take time to see the spirit of a person and not be blinded by their representative, see all you have to do is give it some time and soon a leopard will reveal its spots. However, I didn't do that, I assumed everyone was integral, loving and loyal like me and it cost me much heartache. If I didn't know how Jesus felt emotionally in the garden of Gethsemane when he was kissed by Judas, I do now.

Chapter 8- Spiritual Monsters

I got licensed April 8th, 2010 by a female Apostle in Norwalk, CA. Her name was "Apostle Nicki" and she was known in the L.A area for her ministry training center. Many Leaders have gone through her school to receive licensing and ordinations to preach the Gospel, however that's not where we initially met. Apostle Nicki had a daughter who was a lesbian, she was twenty years my senior and we dated on and off when I was fifteen to nineteen. I met "Violet" in a club and lied about my age when I found out she was old enough to be my mom. We got together rather quickly, and she told me that her mother was an Apostle. At that time, I was stripping and escorting, but because I was a hypo-Christian, I didn't want to expose our relationship to her mother. I mean the lady is a whole Apostle for crying out loud, don't introduce me as your girlfriend. So, we lied and said we were co-workers. Oddly, Apostle Nikki and I hit it off right away, I loved her spirit. She was so nurturing and gave me that mother-daughter affection. I would find myself going to see Apostle Nikki more than Violet. Even though I was a wild child I would sit at her feet and listen to her sermons, I'd help her with whatever lesson she was preparing to teach. I truly loved her like a mom, and she loved me just as much, until she found out the truth about me and Violet. We were "outted" by her brother and it broke Apostle Nikki's heart. I didn't lie about it because we were caught. Violet and I were living together, so it was no need to deny it. I not only admitted that I had been sleeping with the Preacher's daughter, but also admitted that I was not her co-worker, but I was a stripper at the time. The close nit relationship had become strained, but Apostle didn't completely throw me away. She would still hug me every time she saw me and pull my short dresses down in that motherly fashion. I kept my distance while I was still with her daughter, just because it didn't feel right. However, Violet and I split after three and a half years. Once I got out the game, the first person I ran to was Apostle Nikki. She was one of the ones confirming that God had called me while I was still wrestling with it. I sat under her ministry and went to the training classes for over a year. She gave me my first mic and platform to not just tell my testimony, but to preach. She was so excited to license me after witnessing where I came from, that's why I was shocked at the change of events in our relationship.

We soon find out that the people we start with are not always the same people we finish with and that was a sad reality for me. I didn't think that would be the case with Apostle Nikki, being that she'd known me since I was fifteen years old and was so proud of my change. When I got out the game, our relationship picked up where it was in the beginning. That closeness and bond redeveloped and she had been my biggest supporter until my ministry grew bigger than what anyone expected. It's one thing to be local and do an interview here and there, but it's another thing to be international, booked and busy. As soon as my story hit the web, I was invited to many different churches, universities, television shows, you name it and the loud praises of my cheerleader became silent.

Something changed in her and in our relationship. It seemed like the more engagements I got, the less encouraging she became. I would call her and ask her for advice on what to do once I arrived and would receive a nice-nasty response. "What? Lil miss celebrity needs advice from me?" I've always been guilty of ignoring red flags and warning signs in order to see the good in people and maintain relationship, so even though she was throwing shade I just took it. I didn't understand why she was upset; I didn't ask for this. In fact, she pushed me into this as she cultivated my gift, taught me the Word and how to run a ministry. It was her that put me on the front line and now that I'm winning the battle you mad? I was dumfounded, but my respect for her kept me close. Despite the unnecessary wedge, I loved her like a mom and a leader, so I was a bit hurt by how she handled me.

Our outings no longer existed, our quality mother-daughter time became few and teaching me how to grow in ministry became null and void. What did I do, was the constant question that crossed my mind? The final straw was when a close mutual person pulled me to the side and told me that Apostle Nikki had made some hurtful statements about me. It was said that she was referring to me as a stripper and not a Minister. She said, "Danielle ain't the only stripper with a story. I've been in ministry over forty years, so it should be me travelling and getting engagements, not her." Something in me knew it to be true, but I still didn't want to believe it. Unfortunately, the person who told me had receipts, so I had no choice but to face the hard truth. First of all, she could have this life, I never chose ministry, ministry chose me. To be honest, if it was up to me, I would've chosen a different path. How do you lose love for me for having the gift you help cultivate? I was confused and hurt, but rejection and failed relationships were something I had become extremely familiar with, so it was painful, yet easy to pull away.

I didn't stay without a covering for long because soon after the disconnect from Apostle Nikki, I was introduced to my Pastor, Bishop Anthony Pigee Sr. I was invited to tell my testimony at his church and became really good friends with his son and daughter-in-law. We all became the best of friends and I kept coming to the church. Bishop Pigee is a real Prophet of God and there was something different about him. He wasn't like the rest of the Preachers I had encountered. In other words, he was more of a parent than a pervert in the pulpit. Instantly, I felt the love of a father, not just spiritually, but naturally. Bishop has six biological children of his own, but still embraced me as a daughter, which meant love and correction also. He didn't care about how big my story was or how many engagements I had, he held me accountable. Till this day, I reverence that man because he was more of a father to me than my natural dad. When I need advice, Bishop gives it. When I'm acting a fool and need correction, Bishop gives it. When I just need a shoulder to cry on, Bishop not only lends his shoulder, but he also finds a solution to the problem. A man full of wisdom and I am blessed to call him dad. I don't even know when we established that he was my spiritual father, I just forced myself in the family and he complied. Bishop married Ron and I and was there for a lot of big life moments. He even prophesied our pregnancy despite what the doctors said, so we were devastated when we decided to leave Los Angeles and go to Atlanta because I didn't want to leave my dad. I refused to join another church or even consider anyone else as a spiritual covering. He would be my father until Jesus said otherwise. However, the distance was a lot to bear. I don't believe in a Preacher not having a covering or someone they are accountable to. My prayer was that the Lord would send someone to continue the work of my Bishop while I was away, and he did!

I posted a video on social media that went viral and it caught the attention of many people including celebrities and mega Preachers. I was contacted by a major voice in the Kingdom. I was overjoyed and at a complete loss for words. She wants to talk to me! This had to be a joke, I said, but it wasn't a joke; this was real, and the moment I heard her voice on the other end of that phone, my heart sank as I listened to her praise me for my boldness. She told me my story captivated her. I was sitting on my bathroom room floor in tears listening to her say she wanted to help me with my ministry. I thought to myself, God had answered my prayers and sent me a living legend! After years of being rejected by Pastors and leadership, this mighty woman of God came in and embraced me in spite of my past, I just knew I was on the Lord's good side if he would allow such excellence to come into my life. Strangely enough, it started off excellent, but I didn't know that I would need a psychiatric evaluation and major deliverance after this encounter.

In the beginning, you couldn't tell me she wasn't Heaven sent. I loved and adored this woman's ministry and I never would have dreamed that she and I would connect, and we didn't just connect, but a bond was built. Outside of her preaching at my conferences and teaching me how to operate in excellence while in ministry, we had a personal relationship and, in my opinion, it superseded our ministry relationship. She had no biological children and the little girl in me still yearned for a mommy. We filled voids for each other, I was a daughter to her, and she was a mother to me beyond a spiritual level. I travelled with her as she fulfilled her ministry assignments. I spent many days and nights at her home. She had other women there that she considered daughters as well and it seemed as if we were a little family unit. My husband was very fond of her as well, so he didn't mind the long trips and everything seemed great, as most things normally do in the beginning.

Because of her greatness and longevity in ministry, people knew who she was and once it was made public that she and I were in close relationship I started getting phone calls. The calls came from other leaders and Pastors warning me about her, as they told me the experiences they've encountered with her and for me to be careful. I heard them out, but I didn't really listen. To be honest I thought some of them were just hating and wishing it were them and not me. Even if she did screw them over or mishandle them, every relationship is different and what you do to one you may not do to the other, so I wasn't shaken by their words. We were so close and connected that I could never see a breach between us. We were good for almost two years and then I met a different person, I guess this was the one everyone had warned me about.

Preaching In Pain

The sweet, but stern, loving mother and mentor suddenly became wicked and mean spirited. The encouragements diminished while the swift rebukes poured in. Nothing I said or did was ever right and she made sure to tell me. I couldn't even catch the Holy Ghost right in her eyes. She told me I shouldn't fall out in the Spirit at my conferences because I was the host, and it wasn't proper etiquette; as if you can choose when the power of God hits you. She requested that I no longer post her on my social media because she wanted to "lay low". I later found out that she was invited to speak on a major platform in Dallas and didn't want to look like she was associated with me, you know the ex-pornstar. I was heartbroken and caught off guard even though I was previously warned about what to expect with her. It seemed like when her career in ministry appeared to be over and the bookings weren't as frequent, she was open to building me and other young women in ministry, but the moment she got her second wind, she changed.

This weird love-hate relationship continued on,

because she was a great manipulator. She'll annihilate you and then try to piece you back together with gifts or an act of kindness. I assumed she had some mental issues because she displayed Bipolar symptoms, but I loved her so much that I endured what most would call abuse. She tore my self-esteem down by telling me I would be nothing without her and people only supported my ministry because of her name. She literally spoke curses over me asking God to dry up everything I touched and to kill me because I offended the Prophetess. She didn't support anything I did if she was not involved in it. Some would ask why would I stay connected to that, and some would think it was because of her celebrity status and wanting to be connected to a big name. Wrong! My strip club days exposed me to many celebrities, in fact they were my clients and I was able to travel and hang out with many athletes, rappers, comedians and unfortunately even Pastors, long before I ever met her, so I wasn't thirsty. Unlike her other "daughters" she had. Some of these chicks behaved like this was a cult, they idolized her and worshipped her because being connecting to her gave them importance and exposed them to a life they didn't have before. Not to mention, they took the mistreatment and verbal abuse because she is a giver and even though she'll tear you apart she'd buy you the world. When you're broke, busted and disgusted, whether naturally or spiritually you'll except dog food just to have a piece of something. A lot of those around her were there for ulterior motive and what was disheartening was that she couldn't tell the real from the fake. I didn't care about gifts or using her name to get ahead, not that I could get far with her name being that it had become tarnished over the years with her many scandals and antics. I genuinely loved her for who she presented herself to be. Flaws and all, I was ten toes down, but she pushed me away with her overwhelming insults and the love me today, hate me tomorrow attitude. She was unstable, but I had sympathy because when a person is constantly betrayed and hurt, they build walls. The unfortunate thing in that is, they don't know those same walls will ruin and destroy God sent relationships.

This was like déjà vu as I was reminded of Apostle Nikki, but this hurt hit different. We were so close, she had no reason to treat me that way and the more she mishandled me, the more I tried to show her love to prove that I accepted her good, bad, and ugly. My love for her was genuine, but instead of my attributes fixing the problem it just continued to get worse. She called me low class and ghetto, she started showing favoritism to her other daughters and they loved it. Many were jealous of our tight nit bond and the moment they smelled a breach, they jumped on it, whispering in her ear about me and fueling her to continue in her foolishness. My "sisters" did anything they could to separate us, but I blame her. Everyone claims to be a Prophet but are blind when it comes to seeing themselves and those around them. She couldn't see that they were jealous and were there for ulterior motives. She couldn't see my genuineness towards her. She couldn't see that she was dead wrong in how she mishandled me and ruined

Preaching In Pain

this relationship, but she's the Prophetess to the nations?

Although, I can't tell you exactly why her heart changed towards me, I can tell you when. She had just finished preaching and as always, I attended. The service had concluded, but she was still in the Holy Ghost. As we were walking, she stopped and said to me, "Get ready for what God is going to do concerning you." She paused, looked at me again and said, "I gotta watch you, because out of all my daughters, you're the one who can take my spot." She then walked away heading into her hotel lobby. After that, things were never the same between us. What spot was she talking about? I didn't care about a spot or trying to be her replacement. I personally don't think any woman can out due what she has done in ministry. To be honest, I wasn't caught all up in the fame of ministry like some of these other folks. After everything that I'd experience I knew every level meant bigger devils and the greater the assignment, the greater the affliction, and I wasn't looking forward to that. Seemed like I was getting a glimpse of Saul and David. David loved and adored Saul and Saul also loved David until jealousy arose. But what did the living legend have to be jealous of? I was no threat nor was this a competition of who will outdo who. I guess she had her prophetic panties on that night and the Lord showed her something in me that I was even unaware of, which upset her.

Why did this keep happening with the female leaders in my life? Whole time I'm looking for motherhood and mentorship for ministry and they keep turning on me. Instead of being spiritual mothers they were spiritual monsters! Although Apostle Nikki changed on me, referenced me as a stripper even after she ordained me and let jealousy or whatever you want to call it settle in, she didn't go this far. Living legend was supposed to build my spirit, but instead she tore it down. I looked up to these older women, but they just looked down on me. I guess I was meant to be a motherless child in the spirit. That's why I thank God for my Bishop Pigee Sr., who continued to father me from afar,

Preaching In Pain

if it wasn't for his love and guidance during those times, I would have been further lost and in jail. There are so many renegade Preachers and here I am longing for accountability while others can't careless about having someone to cover them or keep them accountable. Meanwhile my covering was trying to cut me!

I felt like I was drowning, and I couldn't come up for air. In addition to being torn down by these spiritual monsters, I was still fighting other battles. For many years, I was able to take a licking and keep on ticking, but in this season my arms got tired and I lost this fight.

Chapter 9- Saved & Suicidal

While I continued to do Facebook lives, preach the Gospel and smile, no one knew I was coming apart at the seam. I was running on fumes, but because I'm the "strong friend" and the rock for literally thousands of people, I kept pouring from an empty cup. I kept speaking life into people while I felt like mine was slowly slipping away. I kept giving financially to those in need when I didn't know how I was going to pay my own bills. I continued to pray, preach and prophesy God's word to others, while it was me oh Lord standing

Preaching In Pain

in the need of prayer, but God was silent.

I've dealt with depression and even suicide attempts as a teenager. When the alcohol and drugs wore off, I was forced to face the reality of the degrading lifestyle of porn and stripping. I was forced to deal with my silent storms as I was molested and raped as a child. My sobriety took me to dark places, so I self-medicated to numb the pain back then. However, this time alcohol and drugs were not an option. I could have talked to my Bishop, I could have called my best friends, I could have sat on the therapist couch, but my issues ran deep, and a pep talk wasn't going to fix it. It got so bad that my pain was coming out through my sermons as I titled messages, "God I got questions" and "2017 tried to kill me!" Although, the people were shouting and running around the church because it was relatable, I was not doing ministry. In fact, I was bleeding on the people. I'm not saying there's anything wrong with relatable sermons, however, I was having a public meltdown, and no one noticed it because they were too busy shouting Amen. No one, not the people of God, not my husband, not my closest friends in Atlanta or Los Angeles, not even the Prophets who claim to see everything. No one saw me gasping for air as I was sinking. Maybe I'm to blame for that. Maybe my hard-core exterior and my goofy personality overshadowed what was really going on internally. Everyone thought I was mixing Comedy and Christianity, but in reality, I was laughing to keep from crying. My father would beat the crap out of me when I was little and then dare me to cry. I guess old habits die hard.

At this time, my husband and I had been married for several years and still unable to conceive. I talk about our experience in my second book *Barren*, but what I didn't mention is my frustration with God. I was annoyed and downright angry with him because my personal requests were not to get a big house and a fancy car, all I wanted was to give my husband a son. All this preaching, prophesying and praising I'm doing, all of this persecution I walked through, all the babies that died in me and you mean to

Preaching In Pain

tell me I'm barren? My husband and I would fast, pray and beg God for a son, but year after year it wouldn't happen for us. During disagreements with women whom I considered friends, they would laugh at me and mock me because I couldn't have children, knowing that would knock the wind out of me. I was constantly laying hands and praying for other women and couples to conceive and watching them birth beautiful babies, yet here I was with a dead womb.

We were preparing to tour with the *From Porn To The Pulpit* production. The show did so well in Atlanta, and we all assumed it would have done even better on the road. I took every dime that was made from the first two shows and put it into the next one. The following city was Baton Rouge, Louisiana. I put my cast on a big tour bus, I paid for their hotel rooms, I fed them, and they complained about everything. We showed up to the theater which had twelve-hundred seats, and only fifty people showed up. I was mortified. All my hard work, all my time, all my money down the drain. I had no training in production, I didn't

Preaching In Pain

Sit under famous Directors and Producers to get the blueprint, I didn't have any trained staff in theatre, it was just me doing what God told me to do, so I was at a complete loss as to what to do in a situation like this. However, my actors still performed, and I turned this into a ministry moment and slayed all fifty people in the Holy Ghost. When it was over, the same actors who I paid, fed, prayed for and showed up for even outside of the production, called me out of my name, laughed at me and left me. I considered these people family and did things for them that no other producer had done as they would pull on me with their personal problems and they turned on me and demanded to be paid for the Louisiana show knowing that we took a major loss. My husband and I paid them with our last because there was no money that came in from ticket sales. I scouted for investors and sponsors, but had no luck, so we paid the bus company, the hotels, the actors, the advertisement and the theater out of our pocket until we had nothing left. These same people who just witnessed two very successful shows just a few weeks prior, left me for dead and gave me their butts to kiss after

one failed show. See, people will ride with you as long as you're riding smooth, but the moment you hit a speed bump they'll jump out the car.

This was the time my "armor bearer" Lisa exposed her true motive as well, when she couldn't profit off the Prophet and there was no quick money to be made, she changed too (which I told you all about in *Judas*). She was out of work and she was banking on a quick come up, but God purposely dried up the well. I didn't understand it then, but I later found it when your well runs dry, it'll expose the true nature of those around you.

My husband and I's bank accounts were completely depleted, I'm embarrassed, I'm hurt and the same people I gave an opportunity to just turned on me and left my production all in one night. While all of this was taking place on a Friday night, I had to put it on pause because I

Preaching In Pain

was scheduled to preach in another city the next night. My world is literally crashing, but I had to find a fresh word for the people. I was on the flight with my heart racing and my eyes were swollen from crying so much. I remember getting to the hotel and the host greeted me and wanted to take me to lunch. I pray I didn't leave a bad impression, but I just needed to get to my room because I felt the tears about to fall. They escorted me to my room and the moment I walked through the doors, I collapsed on the bed and the tears were uncontrollable. I cried from the depths of my soul. "God how am I doing your will and you leave me in this position! Barren and broke!" He was still silent. As the time for me to preach was drawing near, every time I would try to write out a word on my paper, my eyes would fill up. I couldn't see my sermon through my tears. I just kept asking the Lord to help me get through this message which he did. I wiped my tears, put on my church face, went downstairs and preached like Jesus was riding on my back. I preached, prophesied, praised, ran around the room, jumped up and down, spoke in tongues just to go back upstairs and cry.

A few days later I had two more speaking engagements in L.A and one happened to be at my home church Life Of Faith. After I finished ministering, my Bishop approaches me and gives me a prophetic word. Now mind you, I never told him the details of what took place in Louisiana. To be honest, I wasn't trying to relive it, but when you have a real Prophet in your life, they'll pick up your spirit even when you're trying to hide it. He gives me the prophetic word on the mic, then whispers in my ear, "I cancel the spirit of suicide." I hit the ground. How did he know? Did my smile not seem genuine? Did I not crack enough jokes or preach hard enough? How did he know I was in zombie mode as I felt like the living dead? I was alive on the outside and well put together, but death was inside of me. When service concluded, we had our father daughter talk, and he lifted my spirits. I didn't know if I was going or coming before I got to him, but God used him to speak life back into me; and then

Preaching In Pain

BOOM! Here comes another hit.

I got back to Atlanta and reality settled in. I saw the subliminal messages that some of the cast posted about me. "I didn't know what I was doing. They were over my raggedy play." One of the male performers who could barely act called me all kinds of whores. I gave him a role because he was a struggling alcoholic and told him this play would save his life. He would always ask me for prayer and scriptures, we never had an issue, but because the show didn't do well, I was a hoe. Here I am broke, not knowing how my husband and I were going to recover, but I made sure every last one of them were paid. Out of a cast of nineteen people, only one refused a check from me. He saw the loss I took in Louisiana and said, "Evangelist, you got us there, put us in a hotel, fed us and had our checks ready. You've done more than enough." He didn't take the money from me and I just cried because they had no idea the position my husband and I were in. The conference a few months prior took a financial hit because I brought in a speaker from the pits

Preaching In Pain

of hell. He came in and demanded thousands of dollars, "preached" with no Bible or notes and raised a total of four hundred dollars. See people think all Preacher's are in it for the money, and that is simply untrue. There were many and are still many days where I have went broke doing ministry events, raised money for the speaker, the singer, the musicians and took nothing. I don't have a bunch of monthly partners or seed sowers; the people who pull on me for prayer and prophecy don't give me a dime. They have given their rent money to mega false Prophets but won't think to give five dollars to the one who genuinely cares about their souls. This man left us in a big hole, but I was part to blame for picking what the people called popular, but lacking power and I paid a heavy cost. We were just getting out of the hole from that fiasco and then this happened. I woke up that morning and my menstrual came, which further upset me. We just did our first cycle of fertility treatments; so, I was excited and hopeful that we were going to get pregnant, but the only thing I was carrying was sorrow. After I informed my Bishop that we'd lost everything in the show, he made sure to give me something that would help with food and gas until Ron got paid. I deposited the check and they took it! The bank claimed I had an old unpaid balance with them from years ago, and out of all days, they decided to take it all that day. That evening, something told me to check my bank account, it was only forty-seven dollars to my name. I couldn't breathe. God are you kidding me right now! Now I got assassin who was disguised as an armor bearer begging for money that she claimed was a seed. All of this was happening back to back and I couldn't take much more.

Word got out to my spiritual monster about the Louisiana show. Even though the relationship had become a little rocky, this was a woman I loved from my soul, she held a special place in my heart, and I thought I was just as special to her. I was hoping that for once, she would be the person I met in the beginning which was loving, kind, nurturing and understanding, but that's only a few of her personalities and they didn't show up that day. The other side of her was monstrous. Instead of her calling to encourage or comfort me at this difficult time, she called yelling and degrading me. She said, "I knew you were going to fail! You'll never be nothing without me! You're stupid. You don't know anything about productions, I knew you wouldn't succeed. You're always going to fail!" After already dealing with so much, these were the last words I heard before I decided that life was no longer worth living.

Cinco de Mayo will never be the same because on May 5th, 2018, I sent suicide texts to two of my best friends, one to my husband and the other to my mother, then I turned my phone off. I got in my car with no seat belt on and drove like a bat out of hell to a nearby cliff. All I did was cry and scream, "Why God! Why?!" It wasn't just the failed show in Louisiana, it wasn't just because we had no money from doing ministry, it wasn't just because the people I helped hurt me, it was everything! Everything I ever walked through since I gave God a yes hit me like a ton of bricks. The persecution from people who didn't feel I was worthy to be in position, the humiliation from my co-workers and internet thugs, the disrespect and lack of acceptance from my husband's family; not being welcomed or included, but actually shunned once I got into ministry by my peers, always being reminded of my past and having it used against me, not being able to birth a child, doors cracked but never completely opened up for me, the betrayals and backstabbing's from my frenemies, constant financial issues due to ministry assignments and always helping others. I never knew what it felt like to be broke until I got saved. I asked God to just send provision for the vision, but it never came. We had to fund everything by ourselves year after year with no help and ministry bankrupted us. I wasn't looking for a come up off of God's people nor was I looking to get rich off of the church, but I didn't want to suffer while doing it either. I'm doing Kingdom work, not selling dope! What's going on here?

Preaching In Pain

Meanwhile, God is quiet through all of this. When it was time for me to prophesy, he spoke loud and clear concerning other people, but when I needed a word for me, silence. I was carrying this weight all of these years and when it got too heavy, my knees buckled. I still tried to hold it together, but when my spiritual monster yelled that I was a failure and I would always fail, it triggered something in me. All of the pain that laid dormant for years sprouted up in full force.

I drove as fast as I could hoping to hit a tree, or a brick wall head on before making it to the cliff. I had every intention on running red lights, which I did, but I didn't want to hurt anyone else on the road, just myself. There was a car in front of me that stopped, and I stopped abruptly behind it. When I looked up, I saw the word EMERGENCY. It was blurry because I could barely see through my tears. It seemed like I was sitting at the light forever, as if God wouldn't let me move. I finally turned into the hospital's parking lot and ran into the Emergency entrance, as I screamed "Somebody please help me! I'm going to kill myself today! Please help me!" I was rushed to the back and approached by an Indian doctor who tried to comfort me. He was nice, but I still wanted to die. When they left me in the room by myself, I took the cord from one of the machine's and wrapped it around my neck. Before it could get good and tight, several nurses and a cop ran in the room. They sedated me and the last thing I remember was being in the back of an ambulance. When I finally woke up, I realized I was in a mental institution, yep a whole nut house. I was being held on a seventy-two-hour suicide watch. I would have much rather woke up in hell, than in this place. I wasn't crazy, well maybe a little bit, but not mental hospital crazy. I was just overwhelmed and fed up with life's constant disappointments and I was tired. Everything came to a head and I could not fight it any longer. I had been the strong one all these years, both in the world and in ministry, now the strong one had become weak. I was weak spiritually, weak mentally, and weak emotionally. It was like my strength had been taken from me and I was wondering how I

Preaching In Pain

allowed it to happen. I took it and endured it all this time, so why now? I guess it's only so much a person can take before they reach their breaking point and I had finally reached mine.

I didn't call anyone because I didn't want to be found. I'm not sure what my plan was once I got out of lockdown; I just didn't want to be found in that moment. Before I could totally vanish, they figured out where I was. Before baby Judas aka Ericka flipped the switch on me, she made some phone calls to her mental health partners and was able to locate me. My husband called the mental ward, and I could hear the tears in his voice. He was relieved that I was still here. The next person I heard from was my mother, I don't think anyone wants to hear or see their mom cry. She just cried and thanked God that I was alive. The next calls came in from my Bishop and my best friends. Seems like everyone was happy I made it except me.

Even though living legend was a monster at this

point in our relationship, a part of me still was holding on to her, still wanting that love and acceptance from her. Call me a fool, but I love hard, until I can't love you anymore. After all the phone calls I received, not one of them came from her. She knew where I was and what occurred, but she never even called to see if I was ok. What she did do was send me multiple emails about how stupid and dumb I was and if she would've known that I was suicidal and weak she would've never chosen me as her daughter. I was taken back by the lack of sympathy being that she was locked up in a straight jacket once before and she was also infertile. I literally walked through the same valley's as her and instead of pulling me in, she threw me away because of it. While I was trying to pick up the pieces of my life, while still wanting death, I'm being called stupid and weak by my "mother". For the most part, I had been very respectful until now. When she said, "And if you really wanted to kill yourself, you'd be dead." I completely lost it and the muzzle on my mouth came flying off. I'll just blame it on the psych drugs they gave me. Most of her "daughters" accepted her abuse and disrespect because they needed her, but I didn't need nobody or nothing, but God to come see about me. That was the last straw for me. Let's forget about our personal relationship, what about having plain old compassion? Where was God in this? She had been in the Gospel for many years, she was no babe in Christ, and this was unacceptable. I'm not a foul mouth Preacher, but during that time I kindly cussed her out and removed her from my life for good.

I was released from the mental hospital after convincing the director that I didn't belong there and that I wasn't going to attempt suicide again. He let me out and my husband was waiting for me on the other side of freedom. We went home and I just laid there staring at the ceiling. God finally spoke to me and said, "If you would've drove over the cliff and hit the water, you would've just gotten wet. If you get a gun and pull the trigger, I'll make the gun jam because you cannot kill purpose." I must admit, I wasn't in the mood to hear that, however it made me feel better to finally hear his voice. Maybe he didn't leave me or forsake me like I had assumed, but I'm still in no mood for this.

I knew I had to work through the depression and revive my spirit. That meant no preaching; I don't know what kind of high or addiction these Preacher's get from being in the pulpit, to the point they won't even sit themselves down to heal. I'm quick to sit down to hear from God and that's exactly what I did. I sat and let real Prophets and Preachers pour back into me. I laid at the Altar to get my strength back. I harassed my Bishop almost daily just to hear the comfort in his voice, but he didn't mind, I guess a missed call from me was better that an obituary. I got back in my Word and let it minister to me, because often times we only study a scripture so we can preach it. After sitting at the feet of Jesus, I finally regained my strength. I was slowly preparing to get back in the ring because I was determined to make the devil pay for this!

Chapter 10-But God

After going through all of that you know I had to get the revelation behind it. Once I got free in my mind and spirit, I was able to actually hear as I communed with God. I talked and he talked back. "Lord what was that?" I said, and the response seemed a bit churchy and cliché at first. "I had to break you to build you." If you could see the look I had on my face, you'd run, but then he broke it down. He said, "Sin built you to act, think, and believe a certain way, so I had to break that off of you to build you into who I wanted you to be. You call it a punishment; I call it a process of promotion!" **Isaiah 64:8** says, we are the clay, and You our potter, and we are the work of Your hand. Even though you were preaching, you were still being processed. I had to mold you into who you were always destined to be. The enemy changed your identity and told you, you were a stripper, a gang banger, a prostitute, etc., but I call you Evangelist; I call you Prophetess, I call you Daughter. I had to get you back to your original state and it was only painful to your flesh. The betrayals, the financial woes, even the illegal relationships I allowed for a season was all a part of a bigger plan. How can you truly minister to what you've never walked through? Some do it, but what I am birthing out of you is authentic. I needed you to first defeat the Goliath's in your life, so you'd know how to slay other people's giants." I was definitely at a complete standstill, but he kept talking.

"First process, you asked, why me? I needed to get you to understand and not fight with why I chose you. You will have enough people to question why I chose you, but I don't need YOU to question your value in me. You viewed yourself from a negative place, that's why you asked, why me? I had to kill your insecurities, but most importantly I had to get you to forgive yourself and see you how I see you.

Next step, you had no support. **Matthew 12:48-49**, says, who is my mother and who are my brothers? And he stretched out his hand toward his disciples and said, here are my mother and brothers! You were looking for support from your natural family which is a common thing to do. However, I needed you to realize that I give righteous replacements. Whatever friend or family member that will not be there to support you or help you with the vision will be replaced by people who will. I'll send you an extended family to call brother or sister, mom or dad as you are already related by my Blood, and I'll send friends to support you as you do my work. You didn't receive support from the people you wanted it from, so I sent you a new people. I needed to change your mindset, I needed you to view things from a spiritual standpoint and not a natural one.

Preaching In Pain

Then you had to deal with Pharisees aka church folks and not being accepted by them. I did that on purpose. I didn't want you to be a part of any church clicks, because church clicks are tainted. They had to reject you so I could keep you pure. I didn't want you getting caught up in religion, and the filth that they think I don't see. You were never supposed to fit in because I created you to stand out! They didn't want you in their pulpits because they didn't want your prophetic gift to pick up on their perversions. They didn't want you in their circles because you are too real and raw, they want to live and look like a lie. They pulled up your movies because they needed something to block out your anointing, so they viewed you by who you used to be and not who you are in me. Don't worry about it, I'll deal with them, but I was allowing it because while it was hurting your feelings, it was building your spirit.

Next process, you were asking for Jehovah-Jireh and that's exactly what I wanted you to do! You made all this worldly money and lived a lavish lifestyle prior to me, you always had a backup plan, but I needed you to not only rely on me, but to trust me. I wasn't punishing you by leaving you in what you call poverty, I was building your faith in me and tearing down your old nature. That old man wanted to rise when it came to financial survival, but I needed to break that mindset. I had to reprogram you to only trust in me as your provider. While you were asking where is Jehovah-Jireh, I was still making ways for you to eat, I was still clothing you, you may not have liked the way I did it, but I was humbling you and tearing down the old arrogance of the hustler in you. Also, people claimed you were doing this for money, and I showed them that you would serve me with nothing in your refrigerator, you would serve me while wearing someone else's clothes, you would serve me while riding the bus, and with no money in your account; this was bigger than what you assumed. You thought I was punishing you financially, but every conference you put on, every show you put on, every book you released was paid for. I was not punishing you; I was processing you.

Preaching In Pain

Next phase, love, lust and infatuation. You fail to realize when you pray the enemy hears you as well and a lot of times the counterfeits come before the real thing. Why? The enemy is a deceiver, and he will deceive you into thinking this person is Heaven sent, when in reality, they came straight from hell. I allowed the fraudulent relationships to come because I was increasing your discernment, again, how can you recognize and slay demons in others if you haven't slayed your own? You need to give single men and women the warning signs. Not to mention, a lot of the relationships you entered were because of impatience and the wrong mindset. You opened yourself up prematurely because you desired to be married and it was for all the wrong reasons. You needed to see when you do it your way it never works, but when you wait on me it'll be just right. Any relationship that I did not put together will bring heavy heart ache. I also allowed them to mistreat you, lie to you, even betray you because you needed to know the difference between an ordained relationship vs lust and infatuation. Not to mention, after all of that it taught you to appreciate the one I gave you.

Next process, persecution. It's simple, **Matthew 10:22** says, and you will be hated by all for My name's sake. But he who endures to the end will be saved. You were loved when you were in the world and full of sin but hated when you came to me. I call you blessed! You did nothing wrong and was persecuted because of your yes. People fail to realize that when they say I want to be Christ-like, one of the experiences in being Christ-like is persecution. **John 15:18** says, If the world hates you, you know that it hated Me before it hated you. I will forever bless you, cover you and protect you because of it. I also allowed it to happen because I needed you to learn how to fight in prayer and not in the streets. Because of your testimony, many people will persecute you, but as a leader you must turn the other cheek and let me fight your battles; just know that I always win.

Preaching In Pain

Next phase, Judas. You and others may not know this, but betrayal makes way for the blessing. Could I have advanced to the next level if there was no Judas? The betrayal is part of the plan. Not to mention, your heart is so pure, which is a beautiful thing, but it can cost you in the end. Your mistake was thinking that everyone has the same heart as you and this needed to happen so you could see out of a different lens. The first Judas experience occurred and instead of being aware, you continued to let your guard down. You'll have to take the same test until you pass it. Second Judas came around while your guard was down, and you purposely ignored the red flags trying to see the good in the wrong people. I'm not saying every time you come across a Judas, it's because of something you missed, some are just sent from hell and some are sent for purpose. Notice after every betrayal a bigger door opened for you. They thought they were hurting you, but they were actually helping you advance to the next level of promotion. Every Jesus needs a Judas.

Preaching In Pain

Now the spiritual monsters were the devil's doing. I sent them to you to help cultivate your gift, mentor you, mother you, teach you and the enemy came in and poisoned purpose. The spirit of jealousy and envy crept in. The spirit of Saul lingers in seasoned leaders, their focus gets altered by the rising of a younger leader and their insecurities rise; it turns into a competition and when they see the younger leader still rising it goes from competition to murder. They try to murder your spirit in hopes to stop you from reaching where they are, but that only provokes me to take you further. You may have to accept that you are a motherless child in the spirit, but fret not, because I gave you an excellent father. Bishop Anthony Pigee Sr. will be all you need to teach, guide and cover you. Stop looking for add-ons when you already have a gem.

I never wanted you to be saved and suicidal, but it happened, now I will turn what the enemy meant for evil around and use it for your good. I understand that you were overwhelmed, I understand you felt like I left you because I was silent, but what I want you to understand is that I did not and will not, nor will I ever allow you to commit suicide. Your life is far more precious than you know. What I am going to do for you and through you cannot be assassinated. Your assignment is big and unfortunately because I have you slaying big demons you will be faced with big attacks; but you've concurred them all. What you considered failures were successes in Heaven. It may have been with blood, sweat and tears but you did it and you will continue to do it. I won't give you more than you can bear. At times it may feel like too much, but I know your strengths. You cannot kill purpose, no matter how heavy it is to carry, you shall live and not die. I have given you my strength to carry out the task and it shall be completed."

One day with God is better than any day without him. His voice, his assurance, his love revived me. I hate to say that it took a breakdown to happen in order for me to breakthrough, but it's true. I had to breakthrough all of the hidden things that I was battling with and I did it. Unforgiveness and shame within myself, I conquered! I accepted that my past had a purpose and no one else could ever use it against me. Even concerning where I was financially, I had to learn to trust that God will provide, as long as he gives me the vision, he will provide. Church folks and persecution, I conquered! The world says if you don't have haters, then you're not doing it right. I have used the negativity that comes my way and turned it into motivation to keep doing what my Daddy told me to do. Love, lust and infatuation, I conquered! I learned my value in failed relationships and then I got swooped up my Boaz. Not only did God send me an amazing husband, but there is no more barrenness; we had our son! Judas and spiritual monsters, I conquered! They taught me a very valuable lesson. I had the fear of rejection from childhood, and when you have a fear of rejection you'll hold on to toxic relationships, you'll turn a blind eye to red flags because you don't want to lose that person. But the devil is a lie! Bye Felicia!

I had to stop and get still so I could hear God. I no longer looked at my trials and tribulations as punishment, but I viewed them as process, progress and purpose. The enemy should've wiped me out when I was on the pole, his biggest mistake was letting me get to Jesus. Now that I'm with the Lord, I'm going to make it a priority to give Hell a headache every time my feet hit the ground! This means war!

Chapter 11 - When I Thought It Couldn't Get Any Worse...It Did.

I write this chapter with tears streaming down my exhausted face. I completed the final edit of this book April 8th, 2020 and was ready to share it with the world, as that happens to be my tenth-year ministry anniversary. However, what was supposed to be a great celebration of my accomplishments in Christ, my defeats of demons, my maturity in ministry, and the celebration of the many souls who were saved turned out to be the worst day of my life. This chapter should have never been written, haven't I gone through enough heartache? Not just in ministry, but in life! I have seen dark days, more than I have written about or shared publicly, but nothing could compare to this kind of pain. This brought me to my knees.

My biological father raised me after he and my mother divorced, and I was daddy's little girl; until he was diagnosed with Bipolar disorder and Schizophrenia. He tried to kill me when I was ten years old; he beat me so badly with a wooden paddle and the buckle of a belt in my face and naked body until I passed out twice and then he tried to drown me in a bath tub. The man I looked at like a superhero violated me and destroyed me, I carried those physical and emotional scares with me all the way into my womanhood, so yes, I had daddy issues. Not to play the victim, but it did play a role in my relationship selections and how I involved myself with men and women to fulfill a void that ultimately could only be fulfilled

Preaching In Pain

by God. However, that all changed after much needed deliverance and once I met "Pops" which happens to be Bishop Anthony Pigee Sr. I was invited to speak at his church by his son Anthony Jr. and there was an instant connection, and an instant bond that formed between us. He quickly went from being a Pastor I looked up to, to being my Shepherd and then being my father, in and out of the pulpit. Some people only have access to their Pastor's or spiritual leaders at church, but this was not the case with Bishop and I. He had several biological children, but you couldn't tell me I wasn't one of them, nor did he or his family ever make me feel like an outsider; they all welcomed me, and we became family.

Bishop would always praise me when I succeeded or was at least striving for perfection, but he also rebuked me and held me accountable which I loved. He didn't care about my followers, or how many platforms I stood on he would check me when I was out of order. He stood with me through the highs and lows of my life. He wiped my tears after the miscarriages. He lent his ear for me to vent about my problems. He gave his shoulder when I needed one to lean on. He prayed my dying spirit back to life on many occasions. He did premarital counseling for Ron and I and would put his head down and laugh as I yelled at both of them because they didn't see my point of view. After I pouted, he asked, "are you done now?" Then would gently and kindly correct me as he prepared me for marriage. I was so happy when he married us, and so was he. He was just there through a lot of important times in my life. It broke my heart when Ron and I decided to leave L.A and move to Atlanta because I didn't want to leave my Bishop or my church. Often times, relocation changes relationship and that was my fear, but Pops reassured me that distance doesn't determine real love. After we moved to Atlanta, I was still in close contact with him, and although I was branching out more into ministry by hosting conferences and revival's I never made a move without him. I was still accountable to him because he was my covering no matter where I was in the world.

Preaching In Pain

After my suicide attempt, he was one of the main ones calling to check on me, but his calls and texts were nonstop. Don't get me wrong, I'm grateful for everyone who was there for me during that time, but it was something different about him availing himself as busy as he was. I was like a little child waiting for my daddy to call and as soon as I heard his voice, I felt a little better. Once I rebuilt my strength, I reminded him of a conversation we would always have, "you know when I make it, I'm going to take care of you." He would always respond with, "Yes I know and I can't wait!" I knew years ago that I wanted to take ministry to the marketplace and turn my testimony into a book and then a movie. As of today, the book has manifested and so has the theatrical production, (we're still praying for the movie,) but I knew that Pops would be the first to know and the first person I would bless. I watched this man be a true Shepherd to his sheep. I watched him make sacrificing for his members. I watched him bend over backwards for ungrateful people, so I begged God to bless me in the marketplace so I could bless the

Preaching In Pain

Prophet. Everyone in the pews wants to talk about church hurt, not realizing or even caring about a Preacher's pain. Many have no idea the blood, sweat and tears of a true leader, so you better believe my heart's desire was to show my Bishop some appreciation and I was hoping that appreciation would have broke the bank! His son Jr. would do the offering every morning and he would say, "If you're writing a check this morning, million is spelled m-i-l-l-i-o-n." I made it my duty to pray and beg God to allow my tithe to be at least one million dollars not just to my church, but to the man of God. I never thought that day would never come.

The world entered into a pandemic in the beginning of 2020, and was officially on a worldwide lock down at the end of March. Everything got cancelled, revival's, conference's, vacation's; all cancelled. In March, no one knew the severity of what was called the Coronavirus and Covid-19. March15, 2020, I flew to L.A and preached what happened to be my last message

Preaching In Pain

for my Bishop. My love, honor and respect for this man was no secret, some people will diss you in public and love on you in private. That's fake love, but my admiration for him was loud, real loud and on March 15, 2020, I publicly reminded him and our church of that and it brought tears to my eyes as I described how incredibly blessed we all were to sit under the leadership of a real man of God. I watched Pops wipe his eyes as he would always get emotional. When service was over, it was time to eat; Bishop loved food lol. My plans were to join them at the restaurant, however, my rental car caught a flat and I had to go exchange it which exhausted me and I was unable to meet them, which has been a regret until this very moment. By the time I was done, it was almost time for our second service. After the guest speaker finished preaching, we entered into a prophetic move and Bishop made his way over to me and one of the things he said was, "God is going to do everything that he promised." Then he continued to prophesy, but it was something different about the word this time, it was almost like a reassuring, its hard for me to explain but it came off differently. When service was over, breaking news came on stating that we were entering into lockdown. I have a young son, so I panicked a tad bit because I didn't need to get stuck in Los Angeles while my child was in Atlanta, so I tried to catch a flight that night. Pops came up to me and said the Preaching In Pain conference may have to be postponed because of the lockdown, but we will make it happen. He was so excited about the conference because it would have been my very first one in L.A, as all my others have been in Atlanta. Not to mention, it was also my ten-year ministry anniversary and he was my biggest supporter. He watched me grow, he watched me mature, he watched me contain my Compton demon; I was very much still hood and a little ratchet when he first met me a decade ago, so he was proud of this moment and so was I. We were disappointed about having to reschedule the conference, but we were definitely going to do it. I considered it an honor to minister for or with him, but to stand there celebrating ten years of servitude with the man who poured into me this whole time meant more than anyone could ever imagine, but unfortunately that opportunity never came.

On my wedding anniversary, March 29th, 2020, I got a call from my brother Jr. stating that Pops was in the hospital. Tears instantly filled my eyes, not because I thought anything bad would happen, but because I was frustrated that I couldn't get to him. They were not allowing family or friends to visit the patients due to Covid-19 and I wanted to drop everything and fly out immediately. Jr told me everything would be ok, and I can come when they release Bishop from the hospital. Days turned into weeks, and I constantly called and texted Jr and my best friend which happens to also be Bishop's daughter-in-law, and the report was always the same, that he was stable, but hadn't been released yet. I had my girls out in Atlanta praying non-stop, I prayed all day and even texted Pops knowing his phone was powered off, but I just wanted him to see my messages when he got his phone back. Although, I was upset, I wasn't

panicking, I still felt a calm in my spirit, there was no alert, nothing indicated that death was approaching. We all felt the same way, like ok he got sick and now he has something new to preach about and tell everyone how the Lord healed his body; so I was taken back when I called Jr. and he said Pops went on a ventilator. Wait a minute God, what's up? How did we go from stable to a ventilator? Ok fine, lets pray harder, lets tarry a little more because even though he was on a ventilator I still knew he would come out victorious. His son called for a nationwide prayer meeting via conference call and hundreds of people joined in to pray for Bishop. A few days later, I was standing in my kitchen and I get a phone call from Jr. "Hey, bro, you got good news?" I said.
He said, "No."

"No? What's wrong?"

"Pops didn't make it sis."

All I could do was scream, "YOU'RE LYING!" As my body hit the floor and the tears ran down my

Preaching In Pain

face. I tried to catch my breath just so I could tell Jr. that I was going to catch a flight and be there with them. He said, ok as his voice trembled and then we hung up. My heart burst in my chest, my back hit my hardwood floor and I just kept yelling, screaming and crying, asking God why! "You ain't never hurt me like this God! How could you!" How could he take him?" I screamed over and over as I gagged and made myself sick. Out of all the leaders who could have died, all the false Prophets, all the perverted Preachers, you take him and leave a bunch of Pastor Peter Pan's in the land?

I have never felt pain like this in my life. I have gone through some horrendous things, but nothing pierced my soul like this. I was devastated, confused, broken, hurt, angry and out of my mind. He was my real-life hero, my example, my breath of fresh air, and you mean to tell me he's dead! I have never experienced death this close and I was losing it. Who do I turn to now? Who is going to cover me now? What about

Preaching In Pain

the promises I made to him? I was just with him three weeks prior; I had even spoken to him while he was in the hospital and had no idea he was there. This had to be the cruelest joke of all time. But no matter how many times I considered this to be a nightmare, it was an unfortunate reality.

I did not sleep for thirty days or more because all I could do was cry. I shut down and totally blocked out everyone. I did not preach, I turned down engagements because what I wasn't going to do was preach the Gospel for a God that broke my heart like this. I quit ministry! I'm not the kind of person that asks for houses, cars and material things, my prayer requests for myself is how can I better please the Lord, keep me so my flesh won't disappoint you, cover me as I fulfill my assignments; see I love God for real so things that I ask for ultimately concerns the Kingdom. There were two things I desired more than anything, and that was to give me a son despite being infertile and to heal my Bishop. Just heal him Lord, if not for me, then for his children and grandchildren. If not for me, then for his wife. If not for me, then for his family and friends, but whatever you do, just heal him. No matter how much we pleaded, prayed, and prophesied, he still transitioned.

I know the Bible says in, **2 Corinthians 5:8** says, we are confident, yes, well pleased rather to be absent from the body and to be present with the Lord. Now I know for a fact and can bet my best wig that Bishop was a true man of God and Heaven is his residence, however I wasn't feeling none of that. Nothing in me wanted to be spiritual, as a matter of fact I was very much in my flesh; and when he died a part of me did too. This broke me in an indescribable way and although I flew to L.A a few times to be close to his family, I eventually had to come back home by myself and deal with this alone. My husband was here, but he was grieving also because that was his Bishop as well. There was a darkness that came over both of us at that time. I no longer wanted to preach because I was angry with God and I was also to unstable to stand before the people. I don't believe in bleeding while leading, I did that before and it led me to suicide, so that is no longer an option for me. When your mental and emotional health is not aligned, the last thing you need is a mic.

I kept turning down preaching engagements, I kept ignoring the call of God's people as their prayer requests were coming in. I still had this woe is me attitude months after Bishop's transition, until God checked me one night. He said don't let your grief turn into witchcraft. I paused, as he said it again and continued to speak. "It's ok to cry, its ok to mourn, but it is not ok to allow grief to turn into rebellion, and what is rebellion? Rebellion is a form of witchcraft. I get it, you're hurting because you don't understand what I am doing, you're in your feelings because you don't understand why I allowed this, but your assignment has nothing to do with your feelings." I was understanding, but still not budging. It wasn't until Jr. called me and said its time for you to start preaching, if I can do it so can you. I was a spiritual daughter who loved and adored this man, but this was his biological son, his Jr., encouraging me to go forth. I have never seen strength like this, until I witnessed his son encourage and uplift people who are mourning over his father. I watched him press through the pain which ultimately encouraged me, and I had to shake myself. I love my spiritual father and I am still devastated at his unexpected passing, but I had to quickly realize who was still the head of my life and what my assignment was. Plus, Pops would not be pleased with where I was and what I was doing. He was a no non-sense man when it came to Kingdom business, he didn't believe in the quitting spirit. I could hear him saying, "Danielle, that's enough now." Can't nobody say my name like him, every time he dragged the "elle" I knew he was serious. He visited me a few times in my dreams letting me know he was still with me. As much as I wanted to use his passing as a legitimate reason to throw in the towel, I'd not only let God down, but I'd disappoint Bishop as well. How can you say you honor someone, and you've learned so much from them, but not walk

Preaching In Pain

in what they've taught you? This man has poured so much into me, and it would be a disrespect to his legacy for me not to fulfill my assignment. So yes, even with tears running down my face I still have to write the books, do the stage-play's, make the movies and preach the Gospel in pain. God never promised us perfect days, he never said we wouldn't be affected by death, divorce or depression; in fact, his Word prepares us for trials and tribulations. This hit me like a ton of bricks, but I have learned that our feelings have nothing to do with our yes. Which means, go ahead and cry, go ahead and pout, go ahead and be angry, but when its all said and done, you'll have to wipe your tears and get back on the battlefield.

I'm in pain, but my purpose is greater and so is yours. Its ok to grieve, but you cannot hold God accountable for things that he doesn't owe us. He owes us no explanation for why he does what he does. We may not like it or even agree with the timing of it, but his ways are not our ways.

Preaching In Pain

Sometimes, the removal of the one you love and adore can be for your own growth. For instance, Bishop was such a father to us all and he had a Pastor's heart, so many leaned on him instead of figuring it out for themselves. Many of us ran to him as a solution before running to God or learning for ourselves. Now, we're all forced to put our big girl/boy panties on and do the work because Pops is no longer here to babysit us. We now have to take the tools he gave us and put them to use. This is for some of you who are currently dealing with grief, just as I am; stop looking at their transition as punishment and look at it as promotion. When a student is in school and they meet a certain teacher, they may get attached to that teacher and want to stay in that class forever, but they cannot. At the end of the term, they have to leave that specific teacher to get promoted to the next grade. They now have to take everything they've learned from their favorite teacher and apply it to their next level. Well, Bishop was my favorite teacher.

I'm wiping my tears in this very moment because

Preaching In Pain

I never thought I'd be writing this chapter in my story. Honor your God given leaders while they are here, soak up every teaching, every word of wisdom and even every rebuke; and when they transition continue to honor their legacy by staying on your post. When Jesus died, the disciples were promoted, and they took everything that he taught them and preached the Gospel. Be encouraged.

My Love Letter To The Minister With The Broken Heart...

I know that was a lot to digest. I wrote this book not to just share my experiences, but to let YOU, yeah YOU, know that you're not alone. I get it, most leaders are not allowed to be vulnerable and we suffer in silence, but I urge you today to break your silence, before it breaks you.

To my **Why Me** saints- I know I'm not the only one with a testimony and some of us are not as comfortable with our past. I pray you get delivered from the unwanted opinions of miserable people. A lot of you remain hidden from your gifts, talents and callings because of shame and guilt. It's because of your dirty laundry, your scandalous past, your darkest secrets that qualified you. God needs to turn your mess into his ministry. ***1 Corinthians 1:27*** But God has chosen the foolish things of the world to put to shame the wise, and God has chosen the weak things of the world to put to shame the things which are mighty. What some people would look down on, God said I can use that! Why you? Why not you! So many are waiting for you to write the book, start the ministry, run that business, open that church and you are hesitant because of what "they" might think. Excuse my French, but to hell with what they think, literally! We send every discouraging, hindering, accusatory spirit back to hell from whence it came! I've learned in my own journey that people will discourage you simply because they don't have the courage and tenacity to do what you've been set out to do. A lot of people want to be you. I pray you get delivered from people and I also pray you forgive yourself. A lot of my unacceptance of who God was calling me to be had a lot to do with unforgiveness, shame and embarrassment from my previous actions. Unfortunately, we can be our worse enemy. The moment you walk in deliverance and true forgiveness will be the moment you'll be like Isaiah shouting, "Here am I, send me!" Your mistakes, your experiences, your losses are somebody else's lifeline. Why not you!

To my **No Support** having saints- I'm going to tell you now, don't look for the support to come from your family and friends. It seems unfortunate, but most of your biggest supporters will be strangers. Why is that? I personally believe it's harder for people who are familiar with who we were to accept the new version of us. If they've known you your whole life as "Lil Pistol" the gang banger or "Cinnabon" the stripper, it's hard for them to disconnect you from who they've grown to know. Yes, they will be happy for your change and your decision to be who God called you to be, but most familiar faces won't support your businesses or ministry events especially if you made the decision to do it full time. While strangers will see it as faith, family will see it as foolishness. See, when God gives you the vision, others may not understand it and its alright, it's not for them to understand because he gave it to you! **Psalm 121:1,** I will lift up mine eyes unto the hills, from whence cometh my help. My help cometh from the Lord, which made Heaven and earth. Not only will your help come from the Lord, but so will your support. Don't worry about if your family and friends don't support your vision, he will send those to help build what he has given you.

To my saints who deal with **Church Folk-** Listen, the saints and ain'ts will for sure have you locked up with a charge. Jesus had to deal with church folks too, they were called Pharisees and

Preaching In Pain

Sadducees. There's nothing worse than an old religious, judgmental spirit in the house of God. I have met some of the nastiest people in church and ministry, and it's really sad. The women didn't like me because of how I looked, the men wanted to prey on me and not pray for me, the older Deacons and Mother's looked at me like I was some kind of alien that didn't belong in their presence. I could be the poster child for church hurt from the time I got saved to the time I came into ministry and even now; people in the church have been beyond disrespectful and demonic towards me. However, I don't use "church hurt" as an excuse to not do what God has commanded me to do. I get it, that usher was nasty to you, that Pastor preached your business from the pulpit and Sister Strawberry sat in your spot, but this is not a pass to punish God. Don't let the stupidity and ignorance of others push you away from the Lord. The "See, that's why I don't go to church now because of the hypocrites," won't be acceptable when you stand before him. There will be people that will mishandle you at school, on your job, but the least place you expect to be mishandled is at church. I get it, but the moment we stop placing the sins of people higher than the glory of God we will be able to push pass the offense. Your boss may be rude and nasty, but you haven't quit your job because of it. Why? Because that check means more than your boss's non-sense. That's the same attitude we must take on in the house of God. Church people are just that, people; and people are flawed in many ways. If God has anointed you or gifted you in any area of your life you have a responsibility to be steadfast, immovable and always abounding in the work of the Lord. **(1 Corinthians 15:58)** Even if you're a believer without a position, you still have an obligation to serve God with your whole heart and you are left with no excuse. Church folk can be mean and evil spirited, but church folk didn't die for you. Church folk didn't bless you, heal you, open doors for you or provide for you; God did that, so don't hold him accountable for fleshly folks.

To my **Where is Jehovah-Jireh** saints- If I may be

Preaching In Pain

honest, I never struggled financially until I got into church and then ministry. As a little girl both my parents and grandparents had great careers and we all know I started hustling at fourteen, so I never had an issue making a dollar or two. Seems like the moment I gave God a yes, all my resources dried up. I had nothing and frustration is not even a big enough word to describe that journey, so I get. I was angry with God about it too, until I got the revelation from it. Could it be that you've depended on yourself for so long and God had to reprogram you? He has to get you to a place where you don't depend on yourself or your familiar resources, but you only depend and trust on him to supply your needs. At the end of the day, the Lord wants the Glory and he will share it with no one, so he can't allow your mom to come through, or your ex-sugar daddy to come through for you, he alone has to be the one in order to get the Glory; and the longer it took me to realize that, the longer I stayed in it. He didn't want me to have that same hustler's mentality, he needed to renew my mind. I was always in survival mode and he had to break all these old habits and he used my pockets to do it. What we see as punishment, he sees as process and promotion. I also thought maybe God is testing me to see if I'll stick with him even when the money ran out, since of course little demon seeds accused me of running to the church as a new hustle. Trust and believe out of all the hustling opportunities out there, a church hustle was definitely not for me. I love God and made a vow to do whatever he asked of me if he saved my life and I was loyal to that. Broke, busted or whatever I was holding on. Will you do the same?

There will be times that he won't fund the very vision he gave you. There will be times he won't show up when you call him; and you still have to trust him even when you can't trace him. **Philipians 4:19** says, but my God shall supply all your need according to his riches in glory by Christ Jesus. He will always provide what you need, he just may not always provide what you want and that's the discomfort. Your wants and desires may not come when you want it or how you want it, but he will provide and even if he doesn't, he's still God. Can he trust you to stay on your post even when the bills are backed up? Can he trust you to do ministry even if the account is in the negative? We are always talking about trusting God, but can he trust us? Whether he answers our prayer for provision, or not would you still go forth? It's uncomfortable, it's painful, and at times it may be embarrassing, but just get through the wilderness of your walk. **Psalm 37:25** says, I have been young and now am old, yet I have not seen the righteous forsaken nor his seed begging bread.

To my saints who are in **Love/Lust/Infatuation-** I feel like most men and women who proclaim to be saved generally want to be married, which is an awesome thing. Where we go wrong most times is when we enter relationships behaving as wives or husbands to people God never intended for us to marry. Another mistake is believing that just because he or she can shout, dance and speak in tongues qualifies them as a candidate for marriage. In case you didn't know, the biggest demons are in church, so to fall for an individual with that as the only quality is an injustice to your soul and well-being. The Bible says in **1 John 4:1**, Beloved, believe not every spirit, but try the spirits whether they are of God: because many false prophets are gone out into the world. I don't care if you met that joker on the altar, you better know what spirit sent him or her there before you open yourself to a deadly soul tie.

Obviously, I've had my share of "relationships" within the church world and I had to learn hard lessons. What I've learned helped me not just in terms of romantic relationships, but even in friendships, do not allow everyone to have close access too fast. I'm not saying be stand offish, I'm not saying be extra deep and spooky when you're approached by someone romantically whether in church, ministry or on the street. What I am saying is, if I had a chance to do it over, I would have used the two main ingredients that most of us lack, discernment and patience. When we see someone who is attractive, and they show interest, especially when we already have a desire to be married, the discerning antennas disappear, and we get caught up in the euphoria of things. Then next thing you know, we're following our heart. **Jeremiah 17:9** says, the heart is deceitful above all things, and desperately wicked: who can know it? We follow our hearts and it sometimes leads us into a brick wall. We lack patience, because we want it right then and there, so we don't take our time getting to know this individual. I promise if you take your time and listen closely, they'll tell on themselves. They'll tell you everything you need to know, and you wouldn't miss it if you were discerning as you were listening. We miss a lot because we be in our feelings and then six months down the line you start noticing what was already there. **Philippians 4:6** says, be anxious for nothing. Newsflash, that includes love.

What will hurt you more than being cheated on,

lied to and even physically hit, is knowing that the person you fell for was sent to destroy you. Sent to destroy your name, your ministry, your business, your influence and everything you've worked so hard for. There is no greater pain than falling in love with your enemy. Someone once told me to never deal with a person who has nothing to lose, because a person with nothing to lose will help you lose everything. Love, lust and infatuation can cost you everything, even your sanity. The enemy is very cunning, and he will use the very thing you like, the very thing that turns you on and gives you butterflies to destroy you. I'm sure a lot of people had no clue that the moment they entertained a pretty smile was the moment the enemy won that round. That's why discernment and patience is key when it comes to dating for marriage.

Also, lets deal with the elephant in the room. Most leaders and just people in the body of Christ have sex issues; whether it be fornication, adultery, same-sex attraction, pornography, masturbation, etc., that seems to be a common denominator. Listen, I don't care how oily you may be, flesh can never be saved; so, if you play with fire you will get burned. I was involved in lesbian relationships since childhood and made the mistake of thinking that because I got delivered and was preaching the Gospel that I was strong enough to entertain other lesbians. No ma'am! The enemy knows what you like and there may be a season where he lays low, but that joker is strategic in his planning. You may be single and just want company next thing you know you having sex on a blow-up mattress. You may be married to the opposite sex, but your same-sex ex is coming to town and just wants to talk, now you're having gay sex in the backseat of your car. You may have been involved with a married man and had the strength to leave, now you need a bill paid and you think you can call him for support, he not only pays the bill but he got your legs spread from Genesis to Revelation. It doesn't take much, that's why we must be honest with our struggles with love, lust and infatuation and be mindful about our decisions.

Preaching In Pain

To my **Persecuted** saints- It's not like we weren't warned. Many scriptures tell us that persecution comes with the territory. In fact, Jesus calls us blessed in **Matthew 5:11** when we are persecuted and it may sound cliché, but that's what I've had to hold on to when I face it. I hold on to his word and in the beginning, it hurt my soul, but after ten plus years of ministry, I've grown thicker skin. You don't have to have a jacked-up past like mine to be persecuted, disliked and disrespected; the mere fact that you gave God a yes is enough to upset hell. The moment you choose to be Christ-like, it doesn't just include being humble and free from sin, it includes being persecuted for his name sake. You can raise nine people from the dead, walk on water, fart rainbows, and people will still find fault with you. What kept me warm at night was **2 Timothy 2:12**, if we suffer (with him), we shall also reign with him. The hardest part is learning how to not react out of your flesh and turning the other cheek, but the sooner you master that, the sooner God can elevate you. There is a prize after the persecution.

To my saints with a ***Judas-*** If you want to be like Jesus, you have to get kissed by Judas. I know you want to believe everyone you meet is like Mary Poppins and you want to believe everyone has the same heart as you, but in reality, those closest to you will betray you and stab you in your front and your back. It is a painful place to be hurt by those you've helped, and by those you least expected to be on the other end of the trigger. The sad thing with betrayal, it's never done by an enemy. **Psalm 41:9**, Even my own familiar friend in whom I trusted, who ate my bread, has lifted up his heel against me.

I used to think that it was my fault that I kept bringing the wrong people close to me; there had to be something wrong with me, but that's not always the case. Judas didn't start off with bad intentions. Judas walked with Jesus for three years, did ministry with him, travelled with him, broke bread with him and then when the right opportunity came, he betrayed him. Does that mean that Jesus wasn't anointed because he picked Judas as one of his disciples? Does that mean that Jesus did something wrong? Absolutely not! Sometimes it takes betrayal to launch you into your next. Judas had no idea he was being used for the Glory of God. A lot of people who you loved, befriended, helped and so forth had no idea that the betrayal was apart of the plan. Every time one of my "friends" betrayed me it birthed something out of me, a new testimony, a new ministry, a new book and a greater prayer life! That hurt drove me to my knees, it made me get back into the face of God, not to pray witchcraft prayers against them, but to pray for myself. Lord increase my discernment; Lord show me what you want me to get out of this. The smaller my circle got the more time I spent with him.

I remember I had a frenemy named "Keisha". We were really good friends at one point, but she got extremely mad at me because my dog pooped on her floor, yes you read that right. She took that moment to tell me how she really felt about me; she made fun of the fact that I couldn't have a baby and told me I wasn't crap and laughed at the fact that I didn't have a close relationship with my family, and made fun of the things I went through as a child, again because my dog pooped on her carpet. I was flabbergasted and dumbfounded, we had never argued or fallen out prior, but it took something so minute to expose her real heart. I recall being in my prayer room crying angry tears because I really wanted to pull up, but I just prayed and God said, "I didn't move you here for friends, I moved you here to focus. I will destroy every relationship that I don't approve of." I kid you not that's exactly what he did too. Everyone I picked as a friend, a brother or sister ended if it wasn't handpicked by God.

Why would God allow us to deeply love and take care of the very people who will ultimately break our hearts? Because we are hardheaded! A lot of times we are so blinded by our personal feelings towards a person that we will ignore the signs, so God will allow it to end in betrayal because that will be the only way for us to let go. **1 Corinthians 15:33**. As he desires to elevate and bless you, he knows he cannot do it with the wrong people attached to you and because soul ties and covenants are so hard to break he will allow your Judas to sprout. Betrayal also teaches us to be more careful, more cautious, more concerned, because we're not as wide open as before. If you haven't already, you will encounter a Judas and it will hurt your heart, but it will build your spirit. Just know, every betrayal has a blessing attached to it.

To my saints with **Spiritual Monsters-** Every time I think about this, I'm reminded of the story of Saul and David in **1 Samuel ch. 18 & 19.** You could never imagine that your mentor, your mother/father, the one you admire and look up to would turn on you, simply because of your gift and anointing. I've learned people will celebrate you as long as you don't surpass them and that is sickening to me. When you're dealing with Prophets or anybody that can see, they become aware of your gifts and talents, sometimes before you do. When that happens, they are mandated by God to train and cultivate. The

Bible says in **Titus 2:3-4,** Similarly, teach the older women to live in a way that honors God. They must not slander others or be heavy drinkers. Instead, they should teach others what is good. These older women must train the younger women. We, the sons and daughters, are to learn and glean from the older men and women, it was never supposed to be a competition. I don't know if they go through a mid-life crisis, or if their ego's gets affected, but something demonic happens and the spirit of Saul is ignited.

It's easy to say you don't need a spiritual mother, father or mentor, but that's not the case. We all need to be accountable and taught by someone; that someone just needs to have the heart of God. Pray that the Lord will send you a leader who will build your spirit and not tear it down, that doesn't mean you reject rebuke, but there is a difference between rebuke or correction, vs abuse. I was spiritually, emotionally and mentally abused by a spiritual monster, but just like David, I survived my Saul...and you can too! Always be prayerful about your covering, even after they come into your life continue to pray and fast for God's protection over the relationship. The enemy loves a breach, so beat him in prayer at all times!

To my **Saved & Suicidal** saints- After enduring, persecution, betrayal, embarrassment, no support, financial woes, etc., nothing compared to feeling like God had forsaken me; and that's when I lost it. In **Psalm 51:11,** even David pleaded with God saying, do not cast me away from your presence, and do not take your Holy Spirit from me. Feeling like God is not with you in the fire is devastating and unmanageable. However, once I stopped being angry at God for allowing me stay in the fire longer than I anticipated, I realized that he was taking me through all of this to prepare me for greatness. Of course, it's not seen as that at the time you're going through, it just feels like God has left you to get beat up by Satan. But the fact of the matter is, the greater the anointing, the greater the affliction and the enemy will put stumbling blocks in your way to get you to forfeit your future. That's why giving up and dying seem like an option, but it's not! Your struggle is so great because you are an enemy to the devil and an asset to God. If the Lord allows you to stay in the ring, it's because he knows you're able to withstand the fiery darts of the devil. You cannot kill what God has instilled. I know it's a heavy weight to carry and you are overwhelmed by it all, but you do not have the permission to die prematurely!

Jonah, Elijah, Jeremiah and Job were Prophets of God and they all had battles with suicide. What I got out of these men of God wanting to die, was that the enemy knows that a few attacks here and there won't stop God's chosen, and in order to shut the mouth of the Prophet you have to kill him! That's why the spirit of suicide lingers over the most anointed of God, but I decree and declare that you shall live and not die! Your help is coming, your load will get lighter and victory shall be yours, you just have to make it. It's ok to cry, but it's not ok to quit!

Father, I honor you, I bless your name, I give you Glory for the things you have done, not just for me, but for your chosen vessels who are reading this book. I thank you that you looked beyond our faults, our mistakes and our flaws and saw the best in us all. Lord on behalf of my brother and sister who is reading this, may you pour out your spirit and fill them up again. Lord may you cover them, protect them, guide them every day of their lives. May you release revelation, knowledge and understanding. Father I pray for supernatural strength to overtake those who are currently feeling weak. You said when we are weak you are strong, and we thank you for your strength. I ask that you saturate my brother and sister in you Glory right now. I pray for an overwhelming peace to come over those who are currently facing anxiety. May you remind them of who they are and who's they are. May you remind them that you'll never leave them nor forsake them. May you speak, so they can be comforted by your words. We thank you now Lord for your amazing grace. We thank you for provisions and promotions. We thank you for chance after chance. Forgive us for having battles with wanting to quit on you and the assignment that you gave us. Forgive us for our mistakes that we made in ministry. Wash us and cleanse us in your Blood. We repent for going astray and we ask for godly restoration. We ask to be refocused on you and the vision that you've trusted us with. We invite you back in, to rest, rule and abide in our spirits, in our homes and in our pulpits.

Now, you dirty devil, I serve you notice that you have no power over the men and women of God! Satan the Lord rebuke you! I loose the warring Angels to break the hands and necks off of every demon that you sent to cause confusion and torment. We know your time is short and you can only do what God allows, but you can't kill us. You are still and will forever be defeated. Jesus is Lord and you are a reject that was kicked out of Heaven and now you are jealous of the position the men and women of God carry. You continue to send attacks and battles, but need I remind you that the victory is ours! The Blood of Jesus is against you and I render you powerless over the men and women of God in Jesus name! Amen.

You are special. You are chosen. You are somebody in God. You are valued and we need you. Now go be great!

In Loving Memory of my hero, my father and at times my friend,

Bishop Anthony Pigee Sr.

Your legacy shall not die...

Made in the USA
Columbia, SC
25 August 2021